The Horse Show

The Horse Show

by
Jennifer Baker

With photographs by Leslie Lane

London
GEORGE ALLEN & UNWIN LTD
Boston   Sydney

First published in 1977

© George Allen & Unwin (Publishers) Ltd, 1977

ISBN 0 04 798001 x Papercased

Printed in Great Britain in 11 on 13 point Baskerville
by Butler & Tanner Ltd, Frome and London

Contents

Illustrations

Chapter 1

What Is a Horse Show?

When and where the first horse show was held, what type of horses took part and how they were judged is something of a mystery since no records survive to tell the tale. It is probable, however, that the old medieval fairs were the forerunners of our present shows, and some kind of competition for horses was almost certainly included as a part of the agricultural country shows that took place in the last century and before. Indeed the Royal Bath and West, one of the best known agricultural shows, was first held in 1777 and no doubt classes for horses were included.

Long before the beginning of this century, however, London, or more particularly the Agricultural Hall, Islington, was the centre of the showing world. Here were held the various breed society shows, with classes for Hackneys, ponies, hunters, hacks and heavy horses. Classes were large and competition was fierce, with most of the exhibits being professionally produced. Rules and judging were stringent and after the preliminary judging had been carried out in each class the exhibits were subjected to a thorough veterinary examination; any animal which failed this test was ineligible to continue in the class. Jumping competitions – or 'leaping classes', as they were known – did not appear on the Islington programme until the late 1870s, however, and then they played only a minor role.

Although Islington was the centre of the serious show and

breed scene, it was the introduction of the International Horse Show in 1907 which really put Britain on the equestrian map. Two knowledgeable and enthusiastic Hackney breeders, R. G. Heaton and Frank Euren, who had visited shows in various parts of the world and had assisted in their running, decided to put on a show in London. After discussion with other famous horsemen of the day it was agreed to hold the six-day show at Olympia and to invite the fifth Lord Lonsdale, the Yellow Earl (so named because of his yellow livery), to become the show's president. The Earl accepted and was for twenty-six years the life-blood of the show, which soon proved to be a spectacle of such elegance and splendour that it became the centre of fashionable London society. The show's arena was designed by a landscape gardener; banks of hydrangeas bordered by grass lined the ring while roses rambled over the trellis work and archways. The dome was draped with blue material to depict the sky and baskets of flowers hung from the ceilings; even the lights had shades. The dress of the audience had to be in keeping with the general splendour of the setting. Full evening dress was the order for the evening sessions, with silk hats and morning coats for the afternoon, while rat-catcher was the appropriate dress for the mornings.

The actual classes of the early days of the International abounded with Hackneys, hunters, cobs, heavy horses and polo ponies, most of them breeding and youngstock shown in-hand, i.e. led and not under saddle; there was a wealth of driving classes covering singles, pairs, tandems, four-in-hands, as well as trade vehicles and costers' turnouts; and twelve jumping classes were included during the week of the show. Even at this very early stage a number of entries were received from overseas and the show went from strength to strength, with classes being added and amended as necessary until the outbreak of the First World War. Six years later the horse population in this country had been decimated, but the International was again staged at Olympia with classes organised much as before, although the emphasis had now shifted to the ridden rather than the in-hand exhibit. Later, displays and parades of hounds, tent pegging, Grand National winners and so on were also included in the programme and the show gained momentum again until the Second World War, when the doors finally closed on Olympia. In 1947 the International changed its venue to the vast outdoor arena of the White City, where, although a different atmosphere prevailed, the show became as popular as ever.

It became so popular, in fact, that two years later it was joined by another big London attraction, the Horse of the Year Show, held, then as now, at Wembley. Whereas the International was more concerned with the show exhibits, the Horse of the Year Show laid emphasis on show jumping and in choosing the horse in each category to be the champion exhibit of the year.

While the London shows continued to gain popularity, other agricultural and county shows, as well as the smaller fixtures, were springing up all round the country. They were, of course, produced on a much less lavish scale than the early Internationals, but their objectives were the same, namely to improve and maintain the quality and standard of the exhibits and to provide a shop window for breeders and spectators alike. This is, after all, the *raison d'être* of the horse show.

The two most prestigious and important shows of the season, apart from those held in the capital, were undoubtedly the Royal Windsor Horse Show, founded in 1944 and held in Home Park, Windsor, and the Richmond Royal, now amalgamated with the South of England Show and held at Ardingly, Sussex, but first held in its own right in 1900 at Richmond. At both of these the emphasis was very much on the pure show animal, whether hack, hunter or pony. A number of in-hand breed classes also appeared in their catalogues as did classes for the harness horse. Show jumping played a minor role. Over the years the pattern has changed somewhat; there are fewer draught horse and harness classes, while classes for trade and costers' turnouts have virtually disappeared. At the same time, show jumping has taken a stronger position, and various displays are staged for the entertainment of a largely non-specialist public.

In spite of economic difficulties, increased motor-traffic on the roads and the spread of urbanisation, more people ride and own horses for pleasure today than ever before. Never during the busy show season, which now with the increase of indoor jumping shows lasts virtually the whole year round, does a weekend go by when a show of one sort or another is not being held somewhere. This book is designed to give the less experienced spectators and exhibitors alike a better understanding of what is expected of each type of exhibit in the ring and what the frequently criticised and much maligned judges are looking for.

Chapter 2

The Show Classes

HUNTERS

Principal among the pure show classes are those for ridden hunters of varying experience and weight-carrying ability. At the larger shows classes are included for novice or four-year-olds, lightweights, middleweights, heavyweights, ladies' and small hunters, as well as the hunter championship. All the larger shows, and many of the smaller ones too, affiliate to the Hunters' Improvement and Light Horse Breeding Society (H.I.S.) and their hunter classes are held under H.I.S. rules and judged by one or more of the Society's panel of recommended judges.

The novice hunter class is open to mares or geldings who have never been awarded a first prize worth £15 or over in any ridden hunter class (with the exception of four-year-old classes in the previous year), working hunter, hack or cob class at any show at home or abroad before the closing date of entries. This is the starting point for the inexperienced hunter and there are no weight or height limitations. Light-weight classes are open to mares and geldings deemed capable of carrying up to 13 stone, while middleweight classes are for mares and geldings capable of carrying over 13 stone and not more than 14 stone 7 lb. Heavyweights are deemed capable of carrying over this weight.

It is not always easy to decide which classification your hunter falls into since the animal's weight-carrying ability depends, apart from his condition and fitness or lack of it, primarily on the amount, density, and therefore strength of bone that the animal has; 'bone' is the measurement taken round the cannon bone just below the knee. A lightweight would be expected to have at least 8 in. and a heavyweight not less than 9 in. There are no height limits in any of these weight classes but all exhibits could be expected to be somewhere between 15·3 h.h. and 16·3 h.h. At the discretion of the judges any hunter in a class which in their opinion is of more than the specified weight may be directed to the next weight class.

Judging for each of the weight classes follows the same pattern as that for novice, four-year-old and small hunter classes. On entering the ring horses are expected to walk round, usually on the right rein. At a signal from the ring steward they trot, and then canter and gallop on request before being brought back to a slower pace and going through the same procedure on the other rein. While they are being put through their paces the judge or judges (at the larger shows there are usually two) watch each animal's performance in order to gain an overall impression as to his action and way of going (i.e. the straightness and freedom of the movement) and whether he can easily move both behind and in front. In a hunter the judge looks for a horse who can gallop on with long raking strides, covering the maximum amount of ground efficiently without expending too much effort, and moving from the shoulder not the knee. The animal should be able to swing his quarters along, getting his hocks well under him and going forward freely into his bridle without taking too much of a hold. The trot should be balanced without too much knee action. Any tendency towards a flicking of the toe is undesirable. He should go equally well on either rein and have an efficient braking system. Any horse who bucks, naps or generally misbehaves will be put well down the line (i.e. towards the bottom of the class).

Following this initial showing the judge will probably have a fairly good idea of his first three or four placings and have a rough idea of those further down the line. He then asks his ring steward to bring the animals into line in the order of his preliminary choice. He takes another look at each animal to see whether he wants to change his mind, before riding as many of them as he thinks necessary. Depending on the size of the show and the number in the class this could be all of them or merely the first row. The ones he doesn't want to ride and who are not likely to figure in the final line-up are then sent out of the ring. At a large show, if there are two judges, one starts riding from the top of the line and the other from the bottom. When riding the animals the judge is assessing which one gives a good balanced ride, how each responds to the aids and which ones are likely to be able to 'stay' for a long day's hunting; above all he is asking himself how each one is likely to perform in the hunting field and whether he himself would like to hunt him.

Having ridden as many animals as he thinks necessary, the judge then asks for each one to be stripped (to have its saddle removed) so that he can assess the conformation. Here he will be looking for a quality, workmanlike 'hunter type', with plenty of scope, who stands four square and 'fills the eye'. To be a little more precise, he will be looking for the following points:

A finely chiselled, quality head, tapering towards the muzzle, and of a suitable size for the rest of the animal.

The eyes should be large and bold and widely spaced. Any tendency towards small, piggy eyes should be avoided since they tend to denote a mean temperament.

The nostrils should be full and free of hair.

The ears, neither too large nor too small, should again be set well apart. Lop ears, although often an indication of a kindly temperament, are not encouraged in the show ring.

The whole head should be well set on to a neck neither too short and thick, which gives insufficient length of rein and an unbalanced ride, nor too long, which tends to make the animal heavy on the hand. There should be no tendency towards a 'ewe' neck; it should be well muscled and arched and be in proportion.

The withers should be fairly prominent and narrow since this assists the saddle to stay in place and avoids any tendency towards a loaded shoulder, which restricts the animal's movement.

The chest, however, should not be too narrow, since this predisposes the animal to brush (to knock one leg against the other); nor should it be too wide, in which case he is inclined to roll along and be short of speed.

A good, sloping shoulder is desirable, since this will give a comfortable ride especially when riding up and down hill.

The body should be deep through the girth since this ensures plenty of heart room and staying power, and a natural girth line ensures that the saddle will stay in place.

Ribs should be well sprung and rounded and of sufficient length to give plenty of space for the lungs, an essential feature for stamina. There should be no suggestion of slackness behind the ribs since this makes it difficult to keep the animal in condition.

The back should be virtually straight, not too short, since although this denotes strength it makes for a rather uncomfortable ride, nor too long, long backs being weak (although mares are allowed a slightly longer back than geldings).

Well rounded quarters are a desirable feature, although sloping ones often denote jumping ability. They must, however, be well muscled since it is the quarters that have the propulsive power to drive the animal forward, and any tendency to be 'split up behind' (underdeveloped inside the thigh) should be avoided.

The legs and feet are the most important part of the anatomy. The limbs need to be straight, the knees big and flat and the forearm and second thigh well developed and muscled. The cannon bones should be short and the same width all the way down from knee or hock to fetlock, with no tendency to be 'tied in below the knee' or 'back at the knee' (when the leg appears to be bent back slightly). The elbows should be free and stand away from the ribs as this allows for free movement. The hocks should be large, clean and well defined and low to the ground, without turning either in ('cow hocks') or out ('sickle hocks'). Fetlocks should be flat rather than rounded and puffy, and pasterns should be neither too long, which makes for a comfortable ride but predisposes the horse to tendon troubles, nor too short and upright, which makes for a bumpy, uncomfortable ride and causes jarring and concussion which again leads to unsoundnesses.

Feet should be of reasonable size, open and composed of good, hard horn and with a good, well-developed frog, and each pair should match in size and shape. Small boxy feet, closed in at the heel, are undesirable and prone to disease, whereas flat feet with thin soles are prone to bruising. Both extremes should be avoided.

The whole animal should present an alert and intelligent picture of a horse who stands over a lot of ground and who has good proportions, since this will enable him to give a good balanced ride efficiently and with the least amount of strain to himself.

Having studied each exhibit from all angles, picked up his feet and run his hand down the limbs to ascertain any bony enlargements such as splints or spavins, or bursal enlargements such as curbs or thoroughpins, heat or swellings, the judge asks for the horse to be walked away from him in a straight line and then turned and trotted back past him. This stage of the judging enables a judge to ascertain whether the horse has straight, true action. The animal should track up, i.e. plant his hind feet in the prints made by his forefeet without dishing (throwing his feet out sideways), plaiting (placing one forefoot across in front of the other), or brushing in front. His movement behind should be equally straight with no tendency to brush, forge (when the hind foot oversteps the forefoot and strikes against the shoe), or to go wide behind. When the horse is walked away from him the judge is also able to see whether there is any tendency towards cow or sickle hocks. If a judge feels that any horse brought before him is not entirely sound he may ask the competitor to remove that animal from the ring, or request that it be vetted for soundness by the show's officiating veterinary surgeon. Over the last year or two there has been a deal of controversy between owners and exhibitors of hunters and the H.I.S. as to whether a hobdayed horse is an unsound horse. For many years hunters who had wind afflictions have been hobdayed and shown with no queries, but, following a season when a big hunter champion was known to have been hobdayed, the H.I.S. brought in a new ruling barring hobdayed horses from the ring on the grounds that a hobdayed horse is unsound. (Horses can go wrong in their wind due to several causes, such as virus infection, bad management or poor conformation. This results in them either becoming thick in the wind or making a noise which can vary from whistling to roaring, the left vocal chord usually being paralysed. The hobday operation involves making a small incision in the throat and stripping back the membranes from that area so that more air can get through to the lungs. The problem, however, lies in the fact that the operation, if done well, is almost impossible to detect since no scar is left and the only indication of the operation having been performed is that it leaves the animal unable to whinny – and well-behaved hunters don't usually whinny in the show ring.)

A Dublin hunter championship winner demonstrates his ability to really gallop, covering the ground with long, raking strides and moving from the shoulder.

The judge, having examined the whole line-up in this fashion, requests that the riders remount and ride round in a small circle while he makes his final selection. He must, of course, make his decision on how each animal performs and looks on the day and not on its potential. It is by no means certain that his final line-up will be in the same order as his provisional selection; he may have spotted some fault in conformation in his provisional first choice that he had not noticed initially or he may have got a better ride out of his third or fourth choice. With his final selection clear in his mind he asks the ring steward to bring them in in the order of his choice and the presentation of rosettes and trophies is then made. A red rosette normally denotes first place, blue second, green third, yellow fourth, pink fifth and white sixth,

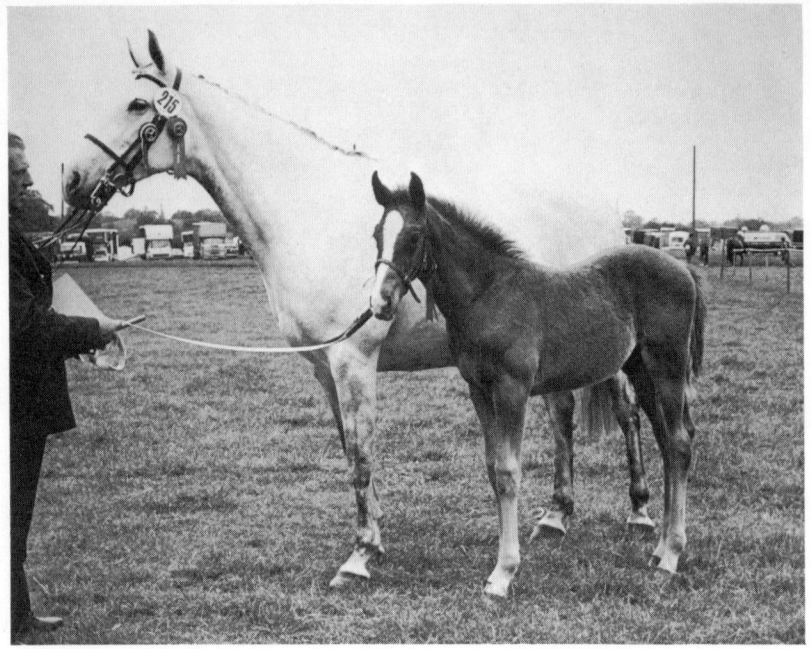

Brood mares are usually shown in a double bridle while foals wear a foal slip.

while championship colours are a composite red, white and blue.

The hunter championship for the best hunter in the show is competed for by the first and second prize winners in the novice or four-year-old, lightweight, middleweight and heavyweight classes. Usually the same judge judges the championship as judged the individual classes and so, although the animals are required to walk, trot, canter and gallop as before, they are not stripped and run out nor are they ridden by the judge. If, however, another judge is called in for the championship he will want to ride those animals who have not already come before him.

The only conditions laid down for a lady's hunter class is that the exhibits should be mares or geldings suitable to carry and to be ridden side-saddle by a lady. No weight or height limitations are enforced but the winner can frequently be a middleweight or lightweight of around 16 h.h. Small hunters are required to be mares or geldings exceeding 14·2 h.h. but not exceeding 15·2 h.h. Judging follows the same pattern as for the weight classes. Neither ladies' or small hunters are, however, eligible to compete for the hunter championship. All hunters are judged on quality, manners, ride, conformation, soundness and action and animals entered in these classes are not eligible, at the larger shows, to compete in either hack or riding horse classes.

In-hand classes are also held for hunters, classes usually being divided by age into those for one-, two- and three-year-olds, as well as those for brood mares and foals. The same quality and action is required as for ridden hunters, although exhibits are only shown at walk and trot, and superficial blemishes do not count heavily against brood mares.

COBS

The cob class is open to mares and geldings not exceeding 15·1 h.h. and capable of carrying 14 stone or over, and is judged on soundness, conformation, ride, quality, action and manners. At the larger shows the class is held under the auspices of the British Show Hack and Cob Association (B.S.H.C.A.) and judged by a member of their panel of judges. The judging of cobs follows the same pattern as that for hunters in as much as they are ridden by both the exhibitor and the judge and then stripped and run out in hand before the final selection is made. However, the cob is a different type of animal and the judge will not be looking for all the same qualities that he would expect to find in a hunter. There is no assured way of breeding a cob; he usually just 'happens', but a small Thoroughbred stallion on an Irish Draught or vanner-type mare will often produce the right sort of horse.

The cob is a utility animal – a stuffy, confidential sort of fellow capable of carrying a great deal of weight.

He is a utility animal and should be able to carry a deal of weight, being small, strong and stuffy. He should have a quality head, and he is almost always shown with a hogged mane. Before the Docking and Nicking Act came into force in 1949, cobs in the show ring were also docked. Sturdy, thick-set and compact, he should stand four square on short, strong legs and have a deep body and wide, well rounded, powerful quarters. Since he must be able to move, straight shoulders are no more favoured in cobs than in hunters. A good length of rein is looked for, with no high knee action, as this will give a good, comfortable, balanced ride. Clean limbs and hard feet are a necessity. He will be required to walk, trot, canter and gallop with free, easy, comfortable paces. The cob is the traditional mount of elderly gentlemen and should be eminently suited to carrying such a rider safely across country. Manners are taken very much into account and any sudden, uncalled-for movements or signs of 'taking hold' should be discouraged. An honest, comfortable, confidential sort of chap, he is – unfortunately – not seen in the show ring as frequently as he was.

HACKS

Although hack classes are held under the same auspices as cobs, namely the B.S.H.C.A., the two are as different as chalk and cheese. The only similarities they share are a necessity for impeccable manners and the fact that hacks, like cobs, cannot be bred as such, but just 'happen'. Four classes are normally held for hacks, as well as the hack championship. These are novice hack, small hack, large hack and lady's hack; a pairs hack class is also sometimes included in the schedule. The novice hack class is open to mares and geldings exceeding 14·2 h.h. but not exceeding 15·3 h.h. who have not won a total of £25 or more in hack classes affiliated to the B.S.H.C.A., lady's and pair hack classes excepted, at the closing date of entries. There are no weight limits in any of these classes.

The judging of hacks takes a somewhat different form from that of hunters and cobs, since in addition to being asked to walk, trot and canter (but not gallop), and being ridden by the judge, horses exhibited are required to give an individual show before being stripped and run out. This show, which should not last longer than 90 seconds, should be designed to show off the animal's paces to the best possible advantage. Movements, which are frequently performed with the reins in one hand, should include the walk, trot, canter, canter out but not gallop, strike off at canter on a required leg, simple change at canter, rein back, stand still and obedience to the leg. Judges are advised to ignore un-called-for movements such as flying changes, performed in order to try to impress them, except in the judging of the championship, when more advanced movements may be taken into account providing, of course, that they are correctly performed. The judging is based 50 per cent on conformation, presence, type and action and 50 per cent on ride, training test and manners.

The majority of hacks are Thoroughbreds, although Anglo-Arabs and part-breds are also frequently seen. However a hack is bred, he must have quality; a small, fine, quality head, a well-shaped neck of good proportions and a good sloping shoulder to give a good length of rein, and a prominent wither giving 'a place to put the saddle'. Like the hunter, he too should have strong loins and be well ribbed-up, and have a good length from the point of the hip to the point of the quarters. Bone, too, is just as important in a hack and less than 8 in. would not be acceptable; neither would any form of blemish. Presence is that indefinable 'something' which an animal either does or does not have; no amount of training can produce it, however beautiful the horse, and it is the quality which will set a good horse above his fellows or, if it is lacking, make a beautiful horse no more than a 'nice horse'. Hack type is not lightweight hunter type, nor is it dressage horse type, nor yet – least of all – a Thoroughbred 'weed'. It is the perfect saddle horse, the pleasure horse, the epitome of elegance. His action, of course, should be straight and true, with no dishing or throwing of legs, and he should move forward freely and gracefully from the shoulder, extending his whole foreleg with only very little knee action. In trot the movement should flow, the foot being brought to the ground after a moment's suspension, with the toe pointed. All gaits should be light and airy with the canter very slow and dainty, the forelegs flicking out and the quarters swinging well under the body. He must give a smooth, balanced ride without being on the forehand or having any tendency towards 'mouthiness',

The hack is the epitome of elegance, the quality riding horse who presents the perfect picture of charm and refinement. Note the formal dress of the rider.

accepting the aids readily without throwing his head about. Manners are all-important in a hack and judges are requested to disqualify any exhibit found to be largely wanting in this department. The whole should present a picture of charm, elegance and refinement and be as near as possible to the perfect horse.

The judging pattern is the same for each of the hack classes: small hack classes are open to mares and geldings exceeding 14·2 h.h. and not exceeding 15 h.h.; large hack classes are open to mares and geldings exceeding 15 h.h. but not exceeding 15·3 h.h.; and lady's hack classes are open to mares and geldings exceeding 14·2 h.h. but not exceeding 15·3 h.h. and suitable to carry and be ridden side-saddle by a lady. The hack championship for the best hack in the show is judged from the first and second prize winners in the novice, small and large hack classes. At the principal shows animals exhibited in hack classes may not be shown in any show hunter, working hunter or riding horse class. Pair hack classes are open to mares and geldings exceeding 14·2 h.h. but not exceeding 15·3 h.h. ridden by a lady and a gentleman. They are ridden together as a pair, the lady riding side-saddle, and the animals should be as perfectly matched as possible, being not only of the same colour and size but also having the same length of stride. Judges take into consideration the similarity of type, their performance as a pair and their turnout.

CHILDREN'S RIDING PONIES

In general terms, the ridden show pony classes resemble those held for hacks in the horse classes. The show ponies come under the auspices of the British Show Pony Society (B.S.P.S.), and it is usual for a novice class, a leading rein pony class and three height division classes to be held, as well, of course, as the championship. At the major shows classes may also be included for a child's first ridden pony, for ponies ridden side-saddle and for pairs of ponies. The child's novice pony class is open to mares and geldings, four years old or over, not exceeding 14·2 h.h., suitable to carry and to be ridden by a child aged 16 or under. He should not have won a first prize in cash valued at £3 or over up to and including the closing date of entries, with the exception of prize winners in the following classes: mountain

A child's riding pony of high quality. Good conformation, manners and temperament are prime considerations in the show pony and must be combined with free forward movement and substance to produce a top quality pony such as this.

and moorland, leading rein, first ridden pony, harness, in-hand, handy hunter, jumping, gymkhana, working pony, pairs, hunt teams, riding school teams and Pony Club teams. The height classes are divided into: mares or geldings, four years old or over, not exceeding 12·2 h.h., suitable to carry and to be ridden by a child aged 12 or under; mares or geldings, four years old or over exceeding 12.2 h.h. but not exceeding 13.2 h.h., suitable to carry and to be ridden by a child aged 14 or under; and mares or geldings, four years old or over, exceeding 13·2 h.h. but not exceeding 14·2 h.h., suitable to carry and to be ridden by a child aged 16 or under.

The judging is similar to that for hacks in as much as exhibitors walk, trot and canter round the ring on both reins, and the two larger height classifications may in addition be asked to gallop, two or three at a time. Competitors in the 12·2 h.h. class are not required to gallop. The ponies are then called into the line in the judge's provisional order of preference before being asked, as in hack classes, to perform an individual show, which should include walk, trot and canter on both reins and probably a gallop and rein back. The show pony should, in fact, move with the same graceful freedom as the hack, although in the smallest of the height classes, 12·2 h.h. and under, where many of the entries will be pure-bred Welsh Section A, the resemblance to the hack action will be less pronounced. Since – unlike the hack, hunter and cob classes – the judges do not ride the ponies, considerable stress is laid on how the pony performs in the individual show, and the judge will notice particularly whether he responds well to the rider's aids or whether he dislikes leaving the rest of the line-up and is inclined to nap and buck. If he does the latter, the judge will – or should – place him right down the line, since manners must be taken into consideration when judging ponies. When each of the ponies has given its individual show, the judge asks for the ponies to be stripped and run out. Again the judge will be looking for similar qualities to those of a hack in that quality and intelligence, good conformation and good manners should be combined with free forward movement and that indefinable spark, presence. But despite the parallel drawn between the riding ponies and the hacks, a pony must never be regarded, much less judged, as a miniature horse. Pony character is an essential element in all three height divisions. The championship is competed for by the first and second prize winners in the novice and the three height classes.

The larger Riding Ponies derive, in the main, from the small Polo Pony stallions, which were usually Thoroughbred, although one famous line descends directly from the pure-bred Arabian, Naseel. In almost every case, however, there will be a background of native pony blood and in the lines not directly attributable to Naseel, a dash of the pre-potent Arabian. The smaller ponies of the 12·2 h.h. and 13·2 h.h. divisions carry a larger percentage of native blood, either Welsh or Dartmoor. Indeed, in the 13·2 h.h. classes a number of entries will be pure-bred Welsh Section B, whilst in the 12·2 h.h. divisions there will frequently be a pre-ponderance of pure-bred Welsh Section A ponies.

The child's first ridden pony is the first class for children off the leading rein and is open to pony mares or geldings, four years old or over, not exceeding 12 h.h., and suitable to carry and to be ridden off the leading rein by a child aged nine years or under. No cantering is allowed except for the individual performance and snaffle bridles only may be worn. Judging takes the same form as for the height classes.

At the principal pony shows, such as the National Pony Society Show and the Ponies of Britain Shows, classes are also held for Riding Ponies in-hand. The quality of their conformation and action is expected to be the same as that of the ridden pony, but the only paces shown are the walk and trot.

The child's side-saddle class is open to mares and geldings, four years old and over, not exceeding 14·2 h.h., suitable to carry and to be ridden side-saddle by a child aged 16 or under. Classes for pairs of children's ponies are open to mares and geldings, four years old and over, not exceeding 14·2 h.h., suitable to carry and be ridden by children aged 16 or under. They should be ridden side by side as a pair and the judges take into consideration the similarity of type and how the two ponies go together. It is therefore sensible to have the pair, both ponies and children, as closely matched as possible.

The child's leading rein pony, suitable for a young beginner to ride.

CHILD'S LEADING REIN PONY

This class is also included at some major shows. The pony must be four years old or over, suitable for a beginner to ride, and not over 12 h.h. Riders must have attained their third but not their seventh birthday. In these classes it is the pony who is being judged on his suitability to carry a beginner; manners and temperament must play a large part. A child's certificate of age, and a measurement certificate for the pony may be required to be produced. At the smaller shows similar leading rein classes are held but frequently the class is judged half on the suitability of the pony and half on the ability of the child rider. In all cases the pony must be led by an adult on foot and in each case the pony will be required to give an individual show at the walk and trot only.

PONY BROOD MARE CLASSES

Classes are also held for pony brood mares, and these are divided into sections for those brood mares with foal at foot and those without foal at foot but with a certificate of service for the current year (which may have to be produced on the day of the show). Foals are judged separately. These are purely in-hand classes, exhibits being required to walk round the ring and to trot when asked to do so, before being brought into line. The object of these classes, as with those for hunter brood mares, is to find the mare most likely to produce the best possible sort of youngstock. Blemishes are not taken into consideration in this class; nor are unsoundnesses providing they are not of a hereditary nature but are the result of an accident.

The wearing of spurs is not permitted in any of the children's pony classes and snaffle bridles only may be worn in the novice class. In each of these classes, where there is an age restriction on the child, the name, address and date of birth of the child must be stated on the entry form before the entry will be accepted.

In the case of children's ponies, hacks, cobs, small hunters, jumping ponies and Hackneys, where height classifications are enforced, competitors may be required to produce an official measurement certificate. The Joint Measurement Scheme, who appoint an official panel of measurers each year, is supported by the British Horse Society, the British Show Jumping Association, the National Pony Society, the British Show Pony Society, the Hunters' Improvement Society, the British Show Hack and Cob Association and the Hackney Horse Society. On payment of a small fee, appropriate height certificates will be issued by members of this panel to owners exhibiting animals in any of these classes. (All animals are measured without shoes.) Life certificates are issued for horses and ponies aged six years or over and annual certificates are issued for animals aged four and five. No certificates are issued for animals under this age. The joint societies recommend that a paragraph be included in show regulations stating that 'Unless measurement certificates issued by the Joint Measurement Scheme are held and produced on request all animals will be measured on the show ground in the shoes in which they are to be exhibited. Half an inch will be allowed for normal shoes.'

Since inches and centimetres do not always relate exactly (except in certain cases such as the 12·2 h.h. pony), the stewards of the Joint Measurement Scheme are recommending that horses and ponies should be measured up to the nearest centimetre when metric measurement takes place in 1980. But the stewards are recommending that measurement in hands and inches should run concurrently with the new metric measurements for some time after the official change-over.

Chapter 3

The Working Classes

A useful class for those animals who have more ability than beauty is that for working hunters. This is the ideal class for hunters who have actually taken their turn in the hunting field and are proved performers rather than for those who, by virtue of their ideal make and shape, have the potential to perform. These working classes also come under the auspices of the H.I.S. and at the major shows two classes are included for them on the schedule, one for lightweights which is open to horses 15·2 h.h. and over capable of carrying up to 13 stone 7 lb. and the other for heavyweights 15·2 h.h. and over capable of carrying 13 stone 7 lb. and over. Where both classes are included there is a championship for the best working hunter in the show, which is judged from the first and second prize winners in both the lightweight and heavyweight divisions. At the smaller shows just the one open class with no weight limitations is usually held.

Working hunters are judged 40 per cent for jumping performance and 60 per cent as for hunter classes, i.e. on ride, conformation and action. The jumping is judged 30 per cent for actual jumping and 10 per cent for style. Fences, of which there should be at least six, should be of a maximum height of 3 ft 9 in., at the discretion of the judges, and should have as natural an appearance as possible in order to simulate the hunting field. They should not be able to be dislodged easily and no coloured poles, such as would be used for show jumps, should be used. Fences composed of straw bales, wattle fencing, brush fences and such like are the sort of obstacles expected.

The jumping section of the judging usually takes place first, horses entering the ring singly to jump the course of fences. The manner of going both of the horse and rider and their freedom in jumping is taken into account. Refusals are heavily penalised. Many judges will penalise a horse more for knocking an obstacle with his front feet than with his hind, since in the hunting field if he knocks fixed fences in front he is likely to land pretty heavily on his nose whereas if he knocks them behind he will come to no great harm. Judges will be looking for a fluent round taken at a good hunting pace and any tendency to 'show jump' fences, for example measuring the stride and 'hooking back', is to be discouraged.

Quite possibly, if the class is a large one of a fair standard, and since working hunter classes tend to be very popular it probably will be, the judge will want to see only those animals who had clear jumping rounds return to the ring for the second part of the judging. This stage follows the same procedure as for the show hunter judging: exhibitors must walk, trot, canter and gallop round the ring on both reins so that the judge can get a general impression of their way of going before he calls them in and rides each of them himself to confirm or reject his initial suspicions. He will not, however, jump them. He will be looking for the same well-balanced ride that he can expect from a show hunter and the same ability to gallop on and yet be easily checked. Horses are then stripped and run out in-hand so that he can assess the conformation and action. Again the same qualities are required as in the hunter, especially in regard to bone and substance, good sloping shoulders for a comfortable ride, depth through the girth for staying power and powerful quarters; but a few honestly-earned lumps and bumps, whilst not to be encouraged, will not be too heavily penalised. When the horses have been judged in this way the riders will remount and circle round the judge until he has made his final selection. They are then called in in order of preference and the awards made.

WORKING HUNTER PONIES

Similar classes are held for ponies who have perhaps not sufficient quality to get to the top in show pony classes but who have the ability to perform across country combined with a degree of quality, conformation and action. These classes come under the auspices of the B.S.P.S. who hold an annual championship show for working hunter ponies with qualifying rounds for these championships being held at the major shows throughout the country. There are three height divisions as in show pony classes, but the pony's height and child's age limitations have been raised to allow the older child and larger pony to compete. The classes are divided into: working hunter pony mare or gelding, four years old or over, not exceeding 13 h.h., to be ridden by a child aged 14 or under, the maximum height of fences being 3 ft; pony mare or gelding, four years old or over, exceeding 13 h.h. but not exceeding 14 h.h., to be ridden by a child aged 16 or under, the maximum height of fences being 3 ft 3 in.; and pony mare or gelding, four years old or over, exceeding 14 h.h. but not exceeding 15 h.h., to be ridden by a child aged 18 or under, the maximum height of fences being 3 ft 6 in. There is also, of course, the working hunter pony championship for the best working hunter pony in the show, judged from the first and second prize winners in the three height classes, and the novice working hunter pony class.

These classes came to this country from America where the emphasis, as in all show classes in the States, is on performance. They were first seen here at the Ponies of

Britain Summer Show where the same height divisions were employed as those for show ponies (12·2 h.h., 13·2 h.h. and 14·2 h.h.); these height limits are still enforced at the Ponies of Britain Show, and the show does not therefore count as a championship qualifier. Although 50 per cent of the marks are awarded for jumping, the 'jumping pony' is discouraged, ponies having won £50 in prize money under B.S.J.A. rules up to the closing date of entries being ineligible to compete. A tough, workmanlike pony with plenty of substance is the type of animal required – the sort that would give a child a good day's hunting. This must be the thought uppermost in the judge's mind when he is assessing each pony. The other 50 per cent of the marks are awarded 10 per cent for style and manners while jumping, 30 per cent for conformation and freedom of action and 10 per cent for manners. Like working hunters, working hunter ponies are usually judged on the jumping section first, the course consisting of no less than a total of five rustic fences as natural-looking as possible. Poor, flimsy and unimaginative fence construction has been one of the chief complaints of this type of class but there has recently been some improvement in this department and those at the annual championship are very inviting, being solid and well built and incorporating such obstacles as dry ditches, tiger traps and water splashes. Marks for jumping are awarded on the same basis as for working hunters, refusals being severely penalised and fences knocked with the hind feet not being as heavily penalised as when knocked with the front. Again the course of jumps should be taken at a good hunting pace and the fences should not be 'show jumped'.

The ponies who have gone clear are then brought back for the remaining stages of judging. As in show pony classes, exhibits are required to walk, trot and canter in both directions before being pulled into line. They are then called upon to give an individual show, which will usually include the gallop, so that the judges, who again do not ride the ponies, can observe more closely each animal in action. Like a show pony, the working hunter pony must be obedient to the rider's wishes and respond readily without napping, but he must also be able to move and should be capable of still being in the hunt at the end of a long day. The pony's conformation should be all that is required in a show pony but with more emphasis placed on bone and substance, perhaps sacrificing a little quality to this end. Superficial marks will not weigh heavily against him but his action must be free and workmanlike with no extravagant paces or flicking of the toe. Once the exhibits have given their show they will be required to be stripped and run out for the judge to make his final decision before they are remounted and the final order announced.

Chapter 4

The Arabian Classes

The Arab is a breed of great antiquity. It is the foundation source of the Thoroughbred and has had an enormous influence on practically every other breed, its blood being very prepotent. In 1918 the Arab Horse Society (A.H.S.) was founded to promote the breeding and importation of pure-bred Arabs and to encourage the reintroduction of Arab blood into light horse breeding, and Arabs have now become so popular that at least one class for them is held at practically every show throughout the country. The A.H.S. holds its own annual three-day show, which is the largest single breed show in the country and includes 66 classes for pure-bred, Anglo- and part-bred Arabs and 18 championships. The first day of the show is reserved for pure-breds and the second and third for part-breds and Anglos.

PURE-BREDS

Pure-breds are defined as Arabian horses in whose pedigrees there is no other than pure Arabian blood. Classes at the breed show are divided by age and sex and again into in-hand and ridden classes. In-hand classes are held for junior yearling colts and senior yearling colts (the difference being the date they were foaled), two-year-old colts and three-year-old colts, junior geldings (open to yearlings, two-year-

Ridden pure-bred Arabians are judged as riding horses. Note that pure-bred Arabs are always shown with the mane and tail loose and flowing, while a narrow leather bridle shows off the well-shaped head to perfection.

olds and three-year-olds) and senior geldings (open to those four years old and over). There are then the same classes, again divided by age, open to fillies, as well as the junior male, junior female and gelding championships which are judged from between the first and second prize winners in the above classes. Junior brood mare classes for mares aged from four to six years with foal at foot, intermediate brood mares aged from seven years up to and including nine years with foal at foot, and senior brood mares aged ten years old and over with foal at foot are each judged in separate classes before the prize winners go forward for the judging of the brood mare with foal at foot championship. Their foals too, although judged at the same time as their dams, are judged separately in their respective classes and a pure-bred Arabian foal champion is selected from the prize winners. Arabian mares aged four years and over without foal at foot have a class to themselves from which the first and second prize winners compete with the brood mare champion for the mare championship title, while the female champion of the show is selected from between the mare champion and the junior female champion. The stallion championship is competed for by the winners of the junior stallion class (for four- and five-year-olds) and the senior stallion class (for six-year-olds and over), the champion then going on to be judged against the junior male champion for the title of the male champion of the show. The other in-hand classes for pure-bred stock at the breed show are the junior male sire produce group and the junior female sire produce group, which is designed to find the sire of the best group. The sire has to be shown along with not more than four and not less than three colts (in the male produce group) or fillies (in the female sire produce group) sired by himself. Foals are not eligible to be shown in this class, the group being comprised of one-, two- or three-year-olds, and each of the animals must be shown, in addition, in its respective class. The sire of each group must be available for service in Great Britain and Eire.

Ridden classes are held for junior geldings aged four, five and six years and senior geldings aged seven years and over (the classes from which the best ridden gelding is judged), junior stallions aged four to six years and senior stallions aged seven years and over (from which classes the best ridden stallion is judged), and Arabian mares of any age. All the exhibits in these classes are judged as riding horses, and the ridden Arabian champion is judged from the first and second prize winners in these three classes.

At the major shows, other than the breed show, Arabian classes are not so numerous. The usual in-hand classes are: Arab mare, open to Arab mares with foal at foot, or due to foal during the current year, or with a certified service during the current year; Arab stallions four years old or over; Arab fillies under four years old; and Arab stallions or colts under four years old. The prize winners in these four classes then go forward to the championship. Only one class is held for ridden Arabs and it is open to stallions, mares or geldings aged four years old or over.

At major shows all classes come under the auspices of the A.H.S. and are judged by a member of their approved panel of judges. In all these classes the judge will be looking for a good stamp of horse who is truly Arabian in character. Admittedly there are variations in type amongst pure-bred Arabians. A Polish Arab, for instance, has a different look about him from a Spanish, and the same is true of an Egyptian-bred Arab when compared with the English 'Crabbet' type. All are accepted as pure-bred Arabians none the less, and each conforms to the general overall character-istics of the breed, although the judge may, of course, have a preference for one type or another.

The principal conformational points in a good Arab are a small, relatively short head, tapering to a 'pint pot' muzzle and with a dished profile. The forehead should be broad and with a slight bulge (known as the *jibbah*) between his eyes, although this tends to be more prominent in mares than in stallions. The eyes should be very large, dark and set rather low in the head and the nostrils, too, should be large and full, while the jowl should be deep and wide. The ears should be small and pricked and set wide apart. The head should be well set on to a rather long, proudly arched neck and there should be no suspicion of a thickness through the throat.

Withers should be fairly pronounced and the shoulder long and well sloped to allow for free movement, although a tendency towards straight shoulders along with poor hind-quarters are the principal faults in the Arab and the ones

which modern breeders are most concerned to eradicate.
The chest should be of a good width to allow for plenty of
heart room and the body should be deep through the girth
with a defined girth line, for staying power. Ribs (the
Arabian is unique in having only 17 pairs compared with
18 in other horses and 19 in some common horses) should
be well sprung and horses should never look as though they
are 'short of a rib'. The back should be short and straight,
or nearly so, with strong loins (another Arabian feature being
that they have only five instead of six lumbar vertebrae)
and with no tendency to a 'goose rump' (a pronounced slope
from the top of the pelvis to the top of the dock). The
quarters should be wide and well rounded and a good length
from the hip to the point of the buttocks and from the stifle
to the hock. The tail, which has 16 vertebrae instead of the
usual 18, should be strong and well set on fairly high up
and carried high and gaily when the horse is moving.

The Arabian has a good reputation for soundness but the
conformation of his limbs and the quality of his feet are an
important consideration. Knees and hocks should be large
and flat. 'Sickle' or 'cow' hocks are severely penalised. The
forearm and second thigh should be well muscled and elbows
should stand well away from the body to allow free and
flowing action. Cannon bones should be short and straight
and any tendency to be 'tied in below the knee', or hock,
is undesirable. All joints should be clean and not puffy and
tendons should be clean and prominent, running parallel
with the cannon. Pasterns should be on the long rather than
the short side and feet should be composed of dense, hard
horn and be of uniform size and shape. Mane and tail hair
should be long and silky in texture and the legs, of course,
clean of feather. Arabians can be found in most colours.
Chestnut and grey are perhaps the most frequently seen,
although bays and browns are also quite common. Blacks
and duns are not seen. Arabians are not divided into height

classifications for showing purposes but their usual height is generally around 14·2–15 h.h.

In addition, Arabians must have equally good action and manners. The paces are similar to those required of a hack. The walk should be free and move from the shoulder, with little knee action and with the hocks well engaged under the body. The trot, which in the Arabian is renowned for its 'floating' quality, should be active, again with the hocks swinging along under the body and driving him forward. As in the hack, the forelegs should reach right forward with a moment's suspension before the foot is brought to the ground, so as to give the distinctive floating appearance over the ground. The tail should be carried high and straight out from the highest part of the back. The canter is the pace at which the Arab excels – light, free, not too fast and supremely comfortable. The general bearing at all times is one of fiery beauty. All action must, of course, be straight and true and any lumps or bumps will count against him, apart from superficial blemishes in the brood mare classes.

Ridden Arabian classes are judged in the same fashion as hack classes; the exhibits are required to walk, trot and canter on both reins before being called into line and then give an individual show prior to being ridden by the judge and then stripped and run out. In-hand exhibits are required to be led round the ring at the walk, usually on the left rein, and when asked to trot to do so individually round the ring. The judge calls them into line in the provisional order and inspects them closely from all angles, running his hands over them, noting any blemishes and so forth. He then requires each one to be walked in a straight line away from him and turned and trotted back straight past him. Having done this with each one, he asks them to walk round again while he makes his mind up as to their respective merits or otherwise before calling them in in their final order.

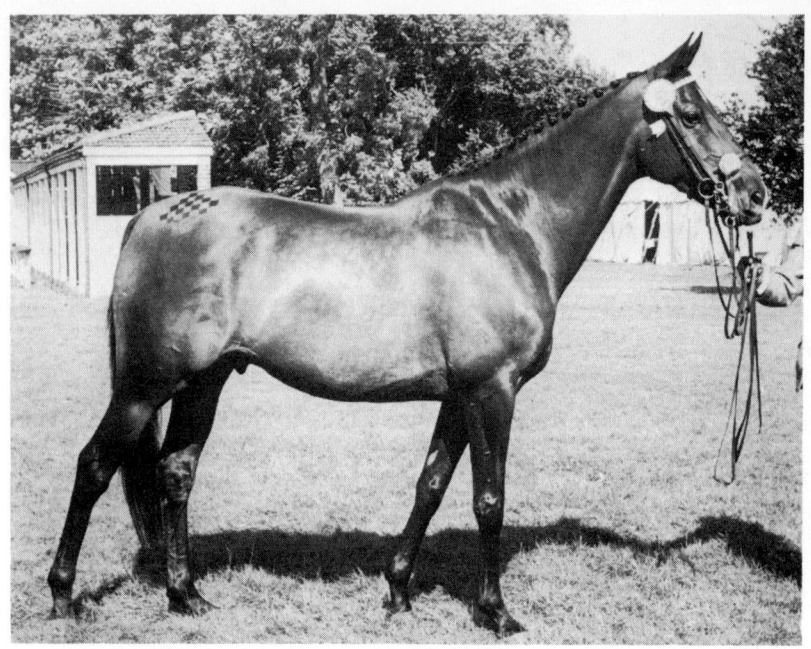

The Anglo-Arab should combine the best points of both parents, the prime considerations being quality and refinement combined with good conformation. This chap is produced and presented in good show condition, well covered but not too fat, with a splendid sheen to his coat and a neatly plaited mane. The chequered markings on his quarters are an added brush mark to catch the judge's eye.

ANGLO-ARABS

Anglo-Arabs are the cross from a Thoroughbred stallion and an Arab mare or vice versa, with their subsequent re-crossing; that is to say they have no strains of blood other than Thoroughbred and Arab in their pedigrees. The Thoroughbred must be registered or eligible for registration in the General Stud Book (G.S.B.) maintained by Weatherbys. Classes are not normally held specifically for Anglo-Arabs at the ordinary shows although there may be a ridden class which is open to pure-breds, part-breds and Anglos. At the breed show, classes are held as follows: Anglo-Arab yearling colts, fillies and geldings, the two highest placed prize winners of each sex going forward to compete in the junior male, junior female and gelding championships respectively. Similar classes are held for two-year-old colts, fillies and geldings and three-year-old colts, fillies and geldings. As before the first and second prize winners of each sex go forward to compete with each other for the gelding championship, junior male championship and junior female championship. Mare classes are divided into brood mares four years old and upwards with foal at foot and mares four years old and upwards without foal at foot, the first and second prize winners of both classes competing with the junior female champion for the female championship. The first and second prize winners in the single class for stallions, four years old and over, go forward to compete with the junior male champion for male championship honours.

Ridden classes are divided by height into two classes, one for stallions, mares and geldings 15 h.h. and under and four years old and over, and the other for stallions, mares and geldings over 15 h.h. and four years old and over. Both classes are judged as riding horses, and the prize winners of each compete together for the overall winning ridden Anglo-Arab. This winner also competes along with the male and female champions and the best ridden part-bred over 14·2 h.h. and under 15 h.h., and over 15 h.h. respectively for the overall Anglo-Arab and part-bred Arab championship.

Theoretically, the Anglo-Arab should combine all the good points of both parents, being the supreme riding horse and combining the beauty and soundness of the Arabian with the extra speed and size of the Thoroughbred. However, the prime considerations are quality and refinement together with conformation. An Anglo-Arab Stud Book is kept by the A.H.S.

PART-BREDS

Part-bred Arabs are defined as horses other than Anglo-Arabs whose pedigrees contain at least 12½ per cent of Arab blood. For animals foaled after 1 January 1974 the percentage has been increased to 25 per cent. Again at the ordinary show, classes are not held for part-breds, but the breed show includes two classes for yearlings; one for colts, fillies and geldings of pony type not likely to exceed 13·2 h.h. at maturity and the other for those exceeding 13·2 h.h. but not likely to exceed 14·2 h.h. at maturity. A similar class is held for two-year-old fillies and geldings not likely to exceed 14·2 h.h., and a composite one for three- and four-year-old fillies and geldings not likely to exceed 14·2 h.h. The winners of these classes go forward to compete in the 14·2 h.h. and under championship. Similar classes, divided by age, are held for colts and geldings of riding horse type likely to exceed 14·2 h.h. at maturity, for two-year-old fillies and geldings likely to exceed 14·2 h.h. and for three- and four-year-old fillies and geldings of the same height, and these too have their championship. Brood mare classes for animals four years old and over with foal at foot of pony type, not likely to exceed 14·2 h.h., and of riding horse type, likely to exceed 14·2 h.h. at maturity, are also held.

Ridden classes are held for mares and geldings over 14·2 h.h. but not exceeding 15 h.h., four years old and over and for those exceeding 15 h.h., while there is also a class for part-bred Arab stallions as well as mares and geldings of 14·2 h.h. and under and four years old and over who are judged as riding ponies. The two larger height winners compete for the best part-bred mare or gelding over 14·2 h.h. championship.

Part-bred classes are difficult to judge since they cover such a wide variety of animals – from show ponies to 'scrubbers' on the one hand and from high-class hacks to

Thoroughbred 'weeds' on the other, some being of really good quality and others being lightweight, light of bone and rather 'flashy'. They are judged on conformation, quality and action, as in any ridden class, the same qualifications being required as for a hack or show pony. Part-breds are eligible to compete in any open riding horse class. A part-bred register is kept by the A.H.S.

Chapter 5

The Mountain and Moorland Breeds

Britain is the only country in the world that can boast of having not one but nine native pony breeds who have roamed these islands for centuries. Each is indigenous to a certain area and each has its own breed society. The National Pony Society (N.P.S.), originally founded in 1893 to promote and improve the breeding of polo and riding ponies and the native breeds, has overall responsibility for all nine breeds. The native breeds are: Dartmoor, Exmoor, Connemara, New Forest, Dales, Fells, Highland, Shetland and Welsh, the latter being divided into four sections: Section A, Welsh Mountain; Section B, Welsh Pony; Section C, Welsh Pony of Cob Type; and Section D, the Welsh Cob. At the principal shows separate in-hand classes will be held for each of the breeds. The more popular breeds (the Connemara, Dartmoor, New Forest, Shetland, Welsh Section A and Welsh Section B) are divided into two sections, one for yearling, two-year-old and three-year-old fillies and colts, and the other for mares and stallions four years old and over. At the smaller shows the breeds will be divided into two categories for mixed mountain and moorland breeds, namely large (Connemara, New Forest, Dales, Fells, Highland, Welsh Section B, C and D) and small (Dartmoor, Exmoor, Shetland and Welsh Section A). At some shows the Welsh

A well-conditioned Dartmoor pony competing in a ridden mountain and moorland class.

Section B will be included in the small division. All ponies must be registered in the stud books of their respective breeds and the registration numbers must be shown on the entry form.

DARTMOOR

Native to the moorland in the south-west peninsula known as Dartmoor, these ponies were used extensively from the 12th to the 15th century to carry tin from the moor down to the towns. At one time there were three distinct herds on the moor, one grey, one dark brown and the third bay; but now blacks, bays or browns are the favoured colours, although all bar piebalds and skewbalds are accepted colours provided they do not have too much in the way of white markings. The height limit since 1924 has stood at 12·2 h.h.

A class of Dartmoor ponies being shown in-hand.

but before that time stallions could be as much as 14 h.h. and mares 13·2 h.h. The average height today is around 11·2 h.h. The head should be small, well set on and fairly short without too much tapering at the muzzle. Ears should be very small and alert and the eyes large and widely spaced. A medium length neck, strong but not too heavy, should join a well laid-back shoulder (i.e. one with a sloping rather than an upright humerus. The back should be neither too long nor too short, strong and well covered in muscle. The body should be deep through the girth allowing for plenty of heart room and the quarters should be strong and muscled, with a good length from the point of the hip to the point of buttock and again to the hock. Limbs should be strong and straight, composed of ample good dense bone and with the forearm and second thigh well muscled. Knees and hocks should be large and flat, and cannon bones short with clean tendons and fetlock joints. Feet should be hard and well shaped with well developed frogs. The mane should be full and flowing, stallions having a moderate crest to the neck, and the tail should be set high and contain plenty of hair. The pony's action should be free, straight and low to the ground with little knee action but without the exaggerated extensions expected from a show pony. The general impression given is of a pretty, well-made, quality pony, sturdily built and with plenty of bone and stamina and described by the Dartmoor Pony Society (D.P.S.) as 'like a miniature middleweight Thoroughbred hunter'.

The D.P.S. has its own section of registered ponies in the N.P.S. Stud Book and also has a Supplementary Register in which there are three grades, S.R., S.R.1, and S.R.2, which was formed for the entry of mares who have been inspected and approved by a panel chosen by the D.P.S. Ponies may only be registered in the stud book if both their parents are so registered or if they are by a fully registered stallion out of a S.R.2 mare.

EXMOOR

Another pony indigenous to the south-west, the Exmoor hails from the moor of that name and comes under the auspices of the Exmoor Pony Society (E.P.S.), which was formed in 1921 to improve and encourage the breeding of Exmoor Ponies. Only three main pure-bred herds now run out on Exmoor, the oldest being the Anchor or Acland herd, and the others being Herd No. 23 and Herd No. 12; but Exmoors are of course bred in many parts of the country. Mares must not exceed 12·2 h.h., while stallions are allowed another inch. The only permissible colours are bay, dun or brown, with no white markings anywhere, and their most noticeable characteristics are the mealy muzzle and the mealy coloured markings round the eyes and inside the flanks. The head should be short and fairly thick with a wide forehead, large, well spaced, prominent and slightly 'hooded' eyes (known as 'toad eyes'), and wide nostrils. Ears should be very small, wide apart, thick and pointed, and the neck should be of a fair length giving a good length of rein. Shoulders should be well laid back and fine at the top, giving an appearance of a wither. The back should be broad and level. The chest should be wide and deep and the ribs long and well sprung, giving depth through the body. Quarters should be powerful with the tail neatly set in and the limbs should be clear, straight, short, and set well apart. Cannon bones should be short and joints and tendons flat and clean and there should be a good length from the hip bone to the hock. The Exmoor coat has a different texture from that of other breeds in that it is harsh and springy in winter – being very dense – and close and bright in summer. There should be an abundance of mane and tail hair and feet should be hard and composed of dense horn. Action should be free and straight, with no exaggerated knee action. Sturdy, intelligent and alert, Exmoors are extremely hardy and stand over a lot of ground.

A pure-bred and first cross register is maintained, the latter being open to ponies with one pure-bred Exmoor parent.

CONNEMARA

The Connemara is a native of Ireland and comes under the banner of the Connemara Pony Breeders Stud Book of Ireland and the English Connemara Pony Society (C.P.S.). They are predominantly grey in colour although black, bay, chestnut brown and dun are also found. They are sturdy, useful animals of between 13 h.h. and 14·2 h.h. and make good riding ponies for both children and adults, being

A splendid Connemara brood mare. Note the quality head, good riding shoulder and good set of limbs.

particularly tractable and agile and of real 'pony type'. They have quality heads with large eyes, well set on to a neck of reasonable length for a good length of rein. Shoulders should be sloping, the body deep through the girth with plenty of heart room and the ribs rounded, well sprung and with no tendency to be 'short of a rib'. Quarters should be muscled and rounded and the back straight and neither too long nor too short. Limbs should be straight and clean, with large flat joints, short cannon bones, a good amount of bone and good hard feet. Action should be that of a quality riding horse: free, easy and low to the ground, with little knee action and with great staying power and an ability to gallop. In recent years there has been an infusion of Arab and Thoroughbred blood into the breed in an attempt to upgrade and, whilst this has resulted in a very attractive and useful type of Riding Pony, the original true type of Connemara has tended to be lost.

A stud book of registered ponies is kept by the N.P.S. and to be eligible for registration ponies must have a fully registered Connemara sire and dam – both being in the stud book – or have not less than 75 per cent of known Connemara blood.

NEW FOREST

As its name implies, the New Forest pony comes from that area of Hampshire known as the New Forest. Since 1938 the New Forest Pony Breeding and Cattle Society has been responsible for improving and maintaining the breed, but as early as 1891 the 'Association for the Improvement of the Breed of New Forest Ponies' was formed in an attempt to improve the breed, and in its wisdom introduced Highlands, Fells, Dartmoors, Exmoors and Welsh as well as Arab stallions to run in the Forest. The result was a bit of a mixture, but for the last 30 or 40 years no out-crosses have taken place and the breed is becoming more uniform in type. Permitted heights are 12 h.h.–14·2 h.h. and any colour other than piebald and skewbald is allowed for registration purposes. The head tends to be rather on the large side, with well-shaped ears, and is set on to a neck which tends to be a little short. This is, however, counteracted by a good sloping shoulder and deep body with well sprung ribs. The back should be straight and strong and the quarters well muscled, while limbs should be straight, clean and hard, with free elbows and good hard feet. They are compact and hardy with plenty of stamina and a deal of quality, making very useful riding ponies for both children and adults.

The N.F.P.B.C.S. publishes its own stud book and recognises a New Forest pony as one 'already registered in the stud book or one known to a member of the council and/or the Agisters as such or one whose dam was a registered pony mare who has run in the Forest for at least one season as a three-year-old or upwards and whose sire was a pony stallion passed by the verderers'.

DALES

The Dales pony inhabits the eastern side of the Pennines in Co. Durham, Northumberland and Yorkshire and is a close relation of the Fell pony. Both ponies were used extensively as pack ponies, transporting lead from the mines out in the hills down to the ports, and also for shepherding. The Dale should not exceed 14·2 h.h. and is black, bay, brown and occasionally grey in colour. Only a limited amount of white markings are permitted, namely a star or snip on the face and socks behind. They are cobby type ponies with a distinctly 'pony' head with a straight or Roman nose. The neck should be of reasonable length although the shoulder tends to be somewhat straight, which does not make for a very comfortable ride. The back should be short and strong, with good strong loins and quarters and legs must be straight with short cannons and a great deal of good dense bone. As with other breeds, joints should be large and flat and the feet hard and open and composed of good horn. Manes and tails should have an abundance of silky hair and the feather, too, should be silky. Dales are particularly noted for their docile, equable temperaments, which make them exceptionally easy to handle.

The Dales Pony Society (Dales P.S.) has its section of registered stock, which is divided into four sections, in the N.P.S. stud book. Section A is for the progeny of fully registered Dales stock who fulfil the Society's inspector's requirements; Section B is for the progeny of fully registered Dales stock who do not qualify for Section A on the grounds of colour or markings; Section C is for progeny of a fully

A Fell stallion. Note the abundance of mane, tail and feather hair. Unfortunately, classes for this breed are usually very poorly filled.

registered Dales stallion and passed by a Society inspector; and Section D is for ponies of unknown breeding but passed by the inspectors as being of Dales type. The Dales Society also accepts progeny of Dales–Fell parentage in their stud book.

FELL

The Fell is found on the northern side of the Pennine range on the fells of Westmorland and Cumberland, and like the Dales was used primarily for shepherding and as a pack pony. The Fell is a little smaller than the Dales, having an upper height limit of 14 h.h. Black is the preferred colour, but bay, dark brown and occasionally greys, with very little or no white markings, are also found. The Fell is more of a riding type than the Dales. It has a small, quality pony head, a good length of rein and a fine sloping shoulder. The back should be straight and is inclined to be a little long, but the body is deep through the girth, with well sprung ribs and strong loins. Quarters are strong and the tail is set a little lower than in other breeds. Limbs must be straight and short with flat, large joints and plenty of good bone. Feet should be good, hard and open. Mane and tail hair should be long, thick and silky, as should the feather on the heels. The action is free with a good long-striding walk, a rather high trotting action and a smooth, flowing canter. Like the Dale, the Fell is very amenable and easy to train. A section of the N.P.S. Stud Book is reserved for the Fell pony, mainly for pure-bred Fell ponies having two fully registered parents.

SHETLAND

Originally the Shetland, the smallest of all our native breeds, came from the Shetland Isles and the far north of Scotland but they are now bred all over the country. They should not exceed 42 in. in height and are more usually about 39 in., no pony exceeding 40 in. at three years old or 42 in. at four years old being accepted for registration. Any colour is accepted, including piebald and skewbald, but blacks are usually preferred. They have small, refined heads with large wide-set eyes and small neat ears. The neck should be well set on to a relatively large body with a short back and strong quarters. He should be well ribbed-up and deep through the girth, with very short legs but plenty of bone. Feet should be hard and manes and tails should be thick and flowing and composed of silky hair, and the general impression is of great strength within a miniature frame. The Shetland Pony Stud Book Society (S.P.S.B.S.) keeps a stud book of registered stock, those eligible for registration being by fully registered parents. Some mares of unknown breeding are accepted for registration after inspection provided they are of Shetland type and have a foal at foot by a registered stallion. No animal is accepted for full registration with the Society until colts are registered as stallions at two years old or over and fillies are registered as mares when they have had their first foal.

HIGHLAND

Bred originally on the Scottish mainland and in the Western Isles, particularly on the Isle of Rhum, the Highland is now bred all over the country. Although the Highland Pony Society (H.P.S.) does not recognise it, it would appear to the observer that there are two distinct types: the heavier mainland type of pony, bred principally for carting deer and probably with an infusion of cart blood some time back, and the smaller Western Isles type of riding pony. The height should not exceed 14·2 h.h. and ponies of the Western Isles type are frequently smaller. Any colour except piebald and skewbald is permissible but grey and various shades of dun are the most favoured colourings, with no white markings allowed. As far as the show ring is concerned there is only one type of Highland. The head should be small and of 'pony' type, with large eyes set well apart and small ears. The neck should be strong and of sufficient length and the shoulders well laid back. The back should be short and straight and the quarters powerful and well muscled. Depth through the heart and well sprung ribs with a nice wide chest are desirable features, as are good strong limbs with short cannons and plenty of bone. Mane, tail and feather hair should be plentiful and silky and an eel stripe down the centre of the back and zebra markings on the lower legs (dark horizontal lines) are frequently seen. Like the Dales and Fells, the Highland is docile and amenable.

The Highland Pony Society keeps its own stud book of registered animals; those eligible for registration have a fully registered sire and dam. Only mares, stallions and geldings three years old or over may be registered. An Appendix A register is open to mares of Highland Pony type if passed by the appropriate inspector; a B register is open to fillies resulting from a cross between a mare in the Appendix A register and a fully registered Highland stallion.

THE WELSH BREEDS

The Welsh breeds are divided into Section A, B, C and D. The Welsh Pony and Cob Society (W.P.C.S.) keeps a stud book of registered stock, those eligible for registration being by fully registered stallions out of fully registered or FS II mares. The FS (foundation stock) Appendices are for mares only who are not eligible for registration in their section of the stud book proper. Progeny of these FS mares are known as FS I, and if put again to a fully registered stallion the progeny are FS II. If the mare is mated again with a fully registered Welsh stallion the progeny are eligible for entry in the stud book proper.

WELSH MOUNTAIN, SECTION A

As its name implies this pony is a native of the Welsh hills where they have roamed for centuries. All sections of the stud book are descended from the mountain pony and all inherit his characteristics. This pony must not exceed 12 h.h. and can be of any colour bar skewbald and piebald, although greys tend to predominate. White markings are not favoured but wall eyes (blue eyes) are not uncommon and tend to be found in the older strains. The head must be small, fine and clearly cut, full of quality and with a slightly

The Welsh Mountain pony, Section A, probably the prettiest of our native breeds.

dished profile. Eyes should be very large, bold and widely spaced, and ears should be very small and pricked. The neck must be well carried and set into strong, well laid-back shoulders. The back should be short, strong and straight with well sprung ribs and the chest wide, to allow plenty of heart room. Loins and quarters should be strong and the tail should be well set on and carried gaily. Limbs should be composed of clean flat bone with plenty of substance, with strong forearms and short cannon bones. Feet should be round, hard and open. Mane, tail and feather hair should be fine and silky. The general impression is one of fiery presence, with good free action, a degree of extension in the paces, and movement being made from the shoulder not the knee.

Judging in progress. A Welsh Mountain pony being examined from all angles.

WELSH PONY, SECTION B

The Welsh pony is a larger version of the Welsh Mountain pony. The maximum height is 13·2 h.h. In the past they were used extensively for shepherding in the Welsh hills and, being tough and strong, were ideally suited for the job. In recent years, with the emphasis on children's quality riding ponies, the Section B has come into his own since he makes an ideal second pony, combining quality and good riding action with native pony type, stamina and good temperament. Any colour except piebald and skewbald is permitted and he should have a neat quality head well set on to a neck of suitable length. The shoulder must be strong and sloping for good riding action, the back level and not too long and the quarters strong with the tail set fairly high.

Substance must not be forsaken for quality and bone should be hard and flinty, with knees and hocks low to the ground and with good hard open feet. The action should be low to the ground, with little knee action, and the paces should be smooth and regular.

Ponies can be registered in the stud book provided they are the progeny of fully registered Section B parents or by Section A stallions out of fully registered Section B mares or out of Section A or B FS II mares.

WELSH PONY OF COB TYPE, SECTION C

The smaller version of the Welsh Cob, the Section C also has a height limit of 13·2 h.h. but is a strong, cobby, stuffy chap, combining strength with quality. He, too, can be of any colour except piebald and skewbald. He should have a well laid-back shoulder and a decent length of rein, giving a good front and making for a comfortable ride. Quarters should be powerful and he should be well ribbed-up with depth through the body. He should have a good amount of hard, dense bone, large flat knees and hocks low to the ground, and hard open feet. The mane and tail hair should be long and silky and his action should be free but with a higher knee action than that of the ponies.

Section C of the Welsh stud book is open to the progeny of fully registered Section C stock, to those by Section C FS II parents, to those by one Section C parent and the other a Section A, B or D and to those Section A ponies who are of cob type but who have grown too large for the Section A register.

WELSH COB, SECTION D

The Welsh Cob is the largest and strongest of the Welsh breeds and, before motorised transport, did most of the

A Welsh Cob, Section D, stallion at full stretch showing all the fiery presence typical of all the Welsh breeds. Note the single plait behind the ears.

work around the farm, since he is as useful for riding as for driving. There is no upper height limit on the Welsh Cob, Section D, but the majority average between 14 and 15·2 h.h. No colour is barred except piebald and skewbald. The head should be small and with quality, and any tendency towards a Roman nose is frowned upon. A Welsh Cob should combine strength and substance with quality. He should have a sloping shoulder, a good length of rein, a deep body and a wide chest. He should be well ribbed-up and have powerful muscled quarters and thighs. Knees and hocks should be large and flat and close to the ground and there should be plenty of hard, dense bone and good hard open feet. Mane and tail hair should be fine and silky as should the feather at the heel. There must be the utmost freedom of action at all paces, with high knee action; they were known for their ability to trot long distances. With the natural fire, courage and action of all the Welsh breeds they make splendid riding horses and, when crossed with a Thoroughbred, make ideal quality hunters.

A stud book of registered stock is maintained. Animals eligible for registration are by fully registered or FS II parents or Section C Cobs who have grown too large for acceptance in that register.

A part-bred register is also maintained by the W.P.C.S. in which any animal can be registered provided that it has 25 per cent of registered Welsh blood, which can come from any section of the stud book.

Apart from the value of all our mountain and moorland breeds in providing excellent riding and driving ponies not only for children but (the larger ones) for adults too, these ponies provide the best possible foundation stock for breeding anything from top-class show ponies to quality middleweight hunters at a second or third crossing.

In all of the in-hand breed classes judging follows the same pattern. All exhibits are led round the ring at a walk, usually on the right rein, while the judge gets a general idea of the animals he has before him. They are then asked to trot individually round the ring so that the judge can assess their action, before he calls them in in a provisional order of preference. The judge then calls each exhibit out one at a time so that he can have a thorough look at him, run his hands down his legs, pick up his feet and so on, and generally inspect him from all angles. He then asks for the pony to be walked away from him in a straight line, turned and trotted back straight past him so that he can see if he moves straight. Having done this with each exhibit, he then asks them all to walk round again while he finally makes up his mind.

At the smaller shows and also at some of the breed shows, in particular the National Pony Society Show, classes are held for ridden Mountain and Moorlands and also for Riding Ponies. These classes are judged in the same way as any other riding horse class. Exhibitors are requested to walk, trot and canter round the ring on both reins before being called in. They are then required to give an individual show before being stripped and run out, but they are not usually ridden by the judge. Marks are awarded for conformation, action, ride and performance and manners.

Chapter 6

The Minority Groups

SPOTTED HORSES

A certain amount of confusion exists regarding the similarity between Spotted animals and Appaloosas, and although both may have the same characteristics and markings the two are certainly not the same, although it is possible that both had the same ancestors. A few enthusiasts have bred Spotted horses and ponies in this country for many years, but it was not until 1963 that the British Spotted Horse and Pony Society was formed to encourage the breeding of Spotted horses and ponies, to register all animals with suitable markings and conformation and, in time, to establish a pure breed of Spotted and good looking horses and ponies. This Society has now been dissolved and two societies, the British Appaloosa Society for horses of 14 h.h. and upwards and the British Spotted Pony Society for animals up to 14·2 h.h., formed in its stead, since it was felt that 'Appaloosa is now a word of common usage and covers the characteristics of most of the horses of that type bred in Britain'.

Three types of spotted markings are recognised: Leopard (spots of any colour on a white or light-coloured background); Blanket (animals having a white rump on which there are spots of any colour); and Snowflake (white spots on a foundation colour, excluding piebalds, skewbalds and dapple greys). Typical characteristics are white sclera round

A Palomino being shown in Western tack. This colour is very popular with Western enthusiasts.

the eye; bare skin is mottled; manes and tails are often very sparse; and hooves are striped yellowish-white and black or brown in vertical stripes. Draught and heavy vanner types are not accepted.

PALOMINOS

The Palomino is not a breed but a colour type and both colour and conformation and action must be taken into account in judging. The true ideal colouring laid down by the British Palomino Society (B.P.S.) is that of a newly minted gold coin, three shades lighter or darker than this being permissible. The mane and tail must be chalk white, not silver, and only a small quantity of white markings is allowed. The eyes must be dark and wall or blue eyes are not recognised. The colour of the mane and tail hair can alter according to the time of year, age of the animal and so forth, as can the coat colour. Consequently a wide variation of colour, ranging from cream to chestnut to grey, may be seen in Palomino classes. The basis of Palomino judging approved by the B.P.S. is that 'colour and conformation should both be taken into account so that neither an animal of good colour and bad conformation nor one of bad colour and good conformation can win'.

The B.P.S. holds an annual show for registered animals which is open to its members and which includes a wide variety of classes to cover every possible animal of Palomino colouring, both in hand and under saddle, from Mountain and Moorlands to ridden Arabs, and from Western pleasure horse classes to those for veterans.

DONKEYS

The Donkey Breed Society Show is held annually and includes such classes as handy donkey, jumping classes, long reining, ridden classes as well as driving and in-hand classes for all ages from foals to veterans. Smaller shows, however, hold only three or four classes for donkeys. These are for stallions, geldings or colts, mares or fillies, and a harness class for private or trade turnout. At some of the larger shows these classes may be further divided into donkey stallion or gelding four years old or over, donkey mare or mare with foal at foot four years old or over, donkey colt or gelding two or three years old, donkey filly two or three years old, and donkey yearling filly, colt or gelding. There will then be a championship, with the winner selected from the first and second prize winners in each of the classes.

All exhibits, with the exception of those in harness classes, are shown in-hand and the procedure followed is the same

A champion donkey stallion being shown in a smart stallion bridle.

as for any other in-hand class. Exhibits are led round at a walk before being required to trot round the ring singly, after which they are called in in the provisional order of merit. The judge then looks them over carefully individually before asking for them to be walked away from him in a straight line and trotted back past him so that he can assess the action.

The donkey's head should be wedge-shaped, wide between the eyes, with a small, soft muzzle and ears that are neither too long nor too short and are carried erect without any tendency to 'lop ears'. The neck should be of proportionate length and the back straight and not too long. The quarters should be as muscled as possible and the legs straight with no tendency to 'cow' or 'sickle' hocks, but donkeys are not noted for their good back ends. The shoulder should be as sloping as possible with the distinctive cross-shaped markings down the back and across the wither extending down

The Shire is the largest of the heavy breeds, standing anything up to 18 h.h. Note the abundance of silky feather at the fetlocks.

the shoulder. Knees and hocks should be large and low to the ground and feet should be good and hard and more close in at the heel than those of a horse. The action should be straight and true, moving freely from the shoulder. The donkey may be of any colour. Chocolate and grey are the most popular.

SHIRE

The Shire Horse Society, established in 1878 to promote the Old English breed of cart horse, holds its show annually. In-hand classes for stallions, mares, geldings and yearling and two-year-old fillies, as well as single and pair harness classes, are held. The standard points for Shires as laid down by the Shire Horse Society are:

'A good Shire stallion should stand from 16·2 h.h. upwards, the usual height averaging about 17·2 h.h. and weight
from 18 to 22 cwt when matured without being over done
in condition. He should possess a masculine head, long
and lean, neither too large nor too small with a long neck
in proportion to the body, and a good crest with sloping,
not upright shoulders, wide enough to support the collar,
running well into the back which should be short, straight
and well coupled with the loins. Eyes should be large, well set
and docile in expression and the ears long, lean, sharp and
sensitive. The tail should be well set on and both head and
tail carried erect. The girth varies from 6 ft to 8 ft in stallions
from 16·2 h.h. to 18 h.h. and ribs should be round, deep and
well sprung. He should be wide across the chest with legs
which should be straight, well under his body and well
enveloped in muscle, and the quarters should be long, wide
and full of muscle and well let down towards the thighs.
Good feet and joints are essential, the feet being wide and
big round the top of the coronets with sufficient length in
the pasterns. Hocks must be broad, deep and flat and
tendons clear cut and hard and clear of the short cannon
bone. Eleven inches of flat bone is sufficient although 12½ in.
has been recorded. Fine, straight and silky hair is required
and when in motion he should go with force using both knees
and hocks, the latter being kept close together. He should go
straight and true behind.'

A stallion should be black, brown, bay or grey with no
splashes of large white marks over his body. He should not
be roan or chestnut, although both are permissible colours
for mares and geldings. Mares should have a minimum height
of 16 h.h. and 9–11 in. of flat bone and a girth of 5–7 ft,
while geldings should have 10–11 in. of bone with a girth of
6–7 ft and a weight of 17–22 cwt. Geldings should be well
balanced, very active, gay movers and full of courage, while
mares should have rather more quality with free action.

A pair of Suffolks harrowing the arena between jumping competitions at the Horse of the Year Show. The Suffolk is the smallest of the heavy breeds.

SUFFOLK

This breed is said to date back as far as 1506 although the Suffolk Horse Society was not founded until 1877, with the object of maintaining the purity of the breed. The Society does not hold its own show, but at the annual Woodbridge Horse Show a number of in-hand and harness classes are held for all ages of Suffolk stallions, mares and geldings. At some of the smaller country shows classes are held for two-year-old Suffolk colts, fillies or geldings, and for Suffolk mares three years old and over. The Suffolk is the smallest of the heavy breeds, being only about 16 h.h., and is always chestnut in colour, a small amount of white markings on the face only being allowed. He is solid and compact and has a rather large head and an exceptionally short and deep body, which gives an impression of great power. The chest is very wide and is set into a well laid-back shoulder. The back is short, level and very powerful and the quarters well muscled. The legs should be short with well-muscled fore-arms and thighs, large flat knees and hocks, and short cannons with a great amount of bone. Feet should be large, composed of hard, dense horn, and have very little feather at the heel, what there is being very fine and silky. He is essentially a farm worker and is well suited to the heavy soil of his native county. In spite of his great bulk he must be able to move freely and with good action.

PERCHERON

Originally a native of northern France, the Percheron came to England in the early 1900s. The British Percheron Horse Society was formed in 1919. Stallions should stand no less than 16·3 h.h. and mares an inch or so less. Grey and black are the acceptable colourings, with only a minimum of white markings being allowed. The head should be fairly short and wedge-shaped, the neck thick and the shoulder well laid back with a short level back and powerful quarters. There should be great depth through the girth, the ribs should be well rounded and the chest wide. Legs should be short and well muscled with short cannons and a good amount of hardy flinty bone, and like the Suffolk there should be little or no feather on the heels. Feet should be open and hard and the whole appearance should be one of enormous strength and power combined with activity. The Society holds an annual show for in-hand and harness horses.

CLYDESDALE

The present-day Clydesdale is the result of crossing the native breed of Lanarkshire with imported Flemish stallions who were introduced to supply more substance and bulk. He is the only one of the 'heavy brigade' who has the power and weight-carrying ability without the bulk, and although he stands between 16·2 h.h. and 17·2 h.h. he is not coarse. Black and brown are the usual colours and white markings on the face, legs and body are frequently seen. The head should be of reasonable size with a straight profile and set on to a good length neck. The shoulder should be well laid back, the back level, quarters long and muscular, and limbs well muscled. Clydesdales tend not to be so wide in front as the other heavies and not to have such depth through the body, but they should be well ribbed-up. Feet should be hard and open and there is an abundance of silky feather on the heel. A good amount of flinty bone is a necessity, as is a long free striding action.

Chapter 7

The Driving Classes

Driving classes are divided into four main categories as follows: private driving, Hackney classes, double harness events and combined driving.

PRIVATE DRIVING

Private driving classes come under the auspices of the British Driving Society (B.D.S.) which was founded in 1958 to encourage and assist those interested in driving horses and ponies. Many of the vehicles used today are of historical interest. Driving classes are becoming increasingly popular and appear on the schedule of a number of local and county shows, and in addition the B.D.S. holds an annual show for its members as well as organising a number of non-competitive rallies and meets. The official meets, which include a 3–4 mile drive, are held at the Royal Windsor Horse Show and the British Timken Show.

Private driving classes are open to stallions, mares or geldings of any height, to be shown in single or double harness to a suitable vehicle, trade and commercial vehicles being excluded. Excessive speed is not required and the suitability of the exhibits for private driving purposes will be specially considered. At the B.D.S. and other large shows classes are divided into sections for non-Hackney types, Hackney types, and pairs and tandems of either type. Non-Hackney types,

Competing in a private driving class. The smart grey is being driven to a Skeleton Gig and the whole presents an elegant picture.

as the name implies, are those animals who are of any breed or type other than Hackney, while the Hackney section is not confined to registered or pure-bred Hackneys but is open to any animal showing a preponderance of Hackney blood, action and conformation.

Initially all sections enter the ring together so that the judge can get an overall impression of each of the turnouts and see whether the vehicles are suitable and fit the animal between the shafts. The class is then divided. Exhibits are shown at a trot, which should be free but not too fast, and there must be at least one change of rein so that the judge can see both sides of the turnout. Then he brings them into line in the provisional order of preference. The judge examines each one in detail and is looking for a horse with a neat, alert head and a neck of reasonable length to enable the easy fitting of the collar. The shoulder of a harness horse tends to be straighter than that of a riding horse but a fairly sloping shoulder is preferred since this leads to better and freer action. The quarters must be powerful and well muscled as must the second thigh to ensure that there is plenty of pulling power for uphill work and stopping power for descending hills. Good hard limbs with plenty of bone are a necessity, as are good, hard, open feet. The harness must fit well and special attention will be paid to the fitting of the collar since if it is too small and narrow it will rub the animal and he will not go forward freely in it. A two-wheeled vehicle such as a Gig, Dog Cart or Ralli Car is usually used for a single animal, while a pair are frequently harnessed to a four-wheeled vehicle such as a Phaeton or four-wheeled Dog Cart, and the vehicle's 'appointments' (the whip and the lamp, which should have a white candle in it) are also taken into consideration when judging. All exhibits are required to give an individual show and the judge notes any animal who naps and does not go forward into his collar. He also notes whether the animal moves straight or whether he is inclined to plait or dish. The whole equipage should present a picture of elegance.

In the pairs or tandem section, judging follows the same pattern. A pair must match as perfectly as possible, not only in size, colour and markings, but in make and shape as well, whereas a pair driven tandem, i.e. one behind the other, need not match. If the two animals are of different sizes, however, the smaller one, providing he goes forward well and freely, should be driven in front, since this gives a smarter outline.

A marathon, non-competitive drive of some 5–8 miles is also included in some show schedules and a speed of about 7 m.p.h. is required. Competitors collect in the showground's main ring before going for their drive and return afterwards to the show ring for the presentation of rosettes to all participants.

HACKNEY CLASSES

Several of the larger shows hold one or more classes for Hackney horses and ponies, and the Hackney Horse Society, established in 1883 to promote and improve the breeding of Hackney horses and ponies and driving and harness horses, holds an annual breed show in conjunction with the South of England Show at Ardingly, Sussex. Entries are judged on soundness, conformation, action, style, quality, manners and pace and, with the exception of the breed show where there are a number of in-hand classes, all animals are shown in harness. Classes are frequently divided as follows: novice Hackney pony, open to stallions, mares or geldings not exceeding 14 h.h. who have never taken a first prize of over £10 in value in single harness at any show at home or abroad prior to January in the year of the show; open Hackney pony classes, open to stallions, mares or geldings not exceeding 14 h.h.; and open Hackney horse classes − open to stallions, mares or geldings exceeding 14 h.h. Novice Hackney horse classes are open to stallions, mares or geldings exceeding 14 h.h. who have never taken a first prize of over £10 in value in single harness at any show at home or abroad prior to January in the year of the show. There is then the champion Hackney pony stakes for the title of Champion Hackney Pony of the Show and the same for the Hackney horse. A class is sometimes included for Hackney pairs and tandems which is open to stallions, mares or geldings of any height.

Whether single, pair or tandem, all are harnessed to a very light four-wheeled show wagon, and a breast harness rather than the heavier collar is used. As in the private driving classes, all exhibits are shown at the trot and in a Hackney class the judge will be looking for the very high, fluid gait that belongs exclusively to the Hackney. Although the Hackney does have a naturally strong, high gait, this is

A Hackney pony being shown to a light four-wheeled show wagon. Note the high-stepping action of the Hackney which is quite unlike that of any other breed.

accentuated in training to meet the demands of the show ring. The forelegs must reach right up and out, really stretching forward, and the action behind must be equally far-reaching with the hind legs being brought up close under the body, and the horse taking a strong hold. As with any harness horse, strong powerful quarters and good limbs and feet are most important. All exhibits are required to circle the ring together at trot on both reins and after an initial selection has been made the judge requires each exhibitor to give an individual show before he makes a final decision.

DOUBLE HARNESS EVENTS

This type of event takes a rather different form from the Hackney classes: it is a competition designed to test the skill and ability of the driver as much as that of the horse. These events are usually divided by height into two groups, those for ponies under 14 h.h. and those for animals over this height. The competition takes the form of an obstacle race. A course is composed of sets of markers, with a clearance of not less than 18 in. greater than the track of the vehicle, which are placed at various points round the course. Several turns and changes of direction are incorporated. The driver must complete the course in the shortest possible time without touching or knocking down a marker. For every second over the time allowed for completing the course he incurs one fault; touching a marker carries the same penalty; and five faults are incurred for knocking a marker over. The driver is permitted to have a passenger on board who can direct the way, but he or she is not permitted to dismount during the driving of the course.

COMBINED DRIVING

This is a comparatively new type of competition introduced by the International Equestrian Federation (F.E.I.) in 1970. There are three separate competitions divided into presentation and dressage, marathon, and obstacle course. Marks are carried forward from each competition and added together, the competitor with the lowest total being the winner. This event, for which there are now World and European championships, is designed for teams of four horses. Cleveland Bays, Irish hunters, Welsh Cobs and Hackneys as well as the big German-bred horses such as Gelderlanders, Hungarians and Oldenburgs make suitable teams. This type of event has gained in popularity and classes are now frequently held in addition for teams of four ponies under 14·2 h.h., pairs of horses 14·2 h.h. and over, pairs of ponies under 14·2 h.h., horses 14·2 h.h. and over in single harness and ponies under 14·2 h.h. in single harness. To take part in any of these classes competitors must be members of the Combined Driving section of the B.H.S.

The object of Competition A, the presentation and dressage, is to judge the turnout, cleanness, general condition and impression of the horses, driver, grooms, harness and vehicle. The vehicle must carry the competitor and two grooms, and passengers may also be carried if desired. Entries will be judged at the halt in an arena and are judged on the following: position, dress, hats and gloves of the driver, grooms and passengers, the way in which the whip is held and the horses handled by the driver; the condition, turnout, cleanness, height of pole and spare equipment of the vehicle and the general impression of the whole turnout. Each judge (there may be between two and five) may award a maximum of 50 marks for this section. The total marks are added together, divided by the number of judges and subtracted from 50, so becoming penalty marks. The competitor with the lowest number is the highest placed.

The dressage phase is designed to judge the freedom, regularity of pace, harmony, impulsion, suppleness, lightness, ease of movement and correct positioning of the horses on the move, and the competitor is judged on his style, accuracy and general command of his team. The dressage test includes the walk, collected, extended and working trots, circles, serpentines, halts and a rein back; it is driven from memory in an arena 100 by 40 metres. Judges can award a maximum of 150 marks for this phase, and penalties will be worked out as for the presentation markings.

Competition B, the marathon course, tests the fitness and stamina of the horses and the judgement of pace and horsemastership of the competitor. The course is divided into five sections, three of them being completed at the trot and two at the walk, and there are two compulsory halts of 10 minutes each. In the trotting sections natural or artificial obstacles such as gates, sharp turns, water and steep hills may be encountered and the referee travelling on each vehicle may penalise competitors for going at the wrong pace. Judges at each of the obstacles may award penalty points if the driver puts down his whip, if anyone leaves the vehicle or disconnects the traces, or if the vehicle leaves the penalty zone around each obstacle, turns over or fails to negotiate any obstacle.

The final phase of the competition is the obstacle course, designed to test the fitness, obedience and suppleness of the horses after the marathon, and the skill of the driver. The course must be between 500 and 800 metres long and consist of not more than 20 obstacles. Markers, similar to those used in double harness events, but with rubber balls balanced on top, are used to define the course and the markers must be 12–16 in. wider apart than the outside track width of the vehicle. The course must be driven at an average speed of 200 metres per minute. Penalty marks are incurred by competitors for touching or knocking over a marker, taking the wrong course or exceeding the time allowed, and the competitor with the least faults overall is the winner.

Chapter 8

Classes at the Smaller Show

At the smaller local shows which abound up and down the country, a number of classes will be found on the schedule which do not always appear at the larger county, breed or agricultural shows. Such classes are the family pony, riding class, handy horse or pony, utility horse, riding horse, best condition and turnout, riding club teams and Western classes. These, and probably others too, can be found at some shows and since most of these classes do not fall under the auspices of any recognised body the judge does not have any clear guidelines to follow. How, and on what, he judges the class is very much left to him.

FAMILY PONY AND UTILITY HORSE

These can be dealt with together since the class requirements are virtually the same. Both are open to mares and geldings capable of giving all members of the family a safe and comfortable ride, and although there is no height limit the animal should obviously be neither too small nor too large. All exhibits are required to walk, trot and canter on either rein and in the utility class they may be required to jump a small fence. Since entries for these classes are normally very large, this is one way of sorting the animals out, those who refuse or do not jump freely being swiftly relegated to the back line. In a family pony class the judge may employ a competent child to ride the first few in the line-up just to make sure that the animal is suitable to be ridden by a child as well as by adults. In a utility class the emphasis is laid on the suitability of the horse for the 'average weekend rider' – a vague and rather meaningless phrase which can be taken to cover anyone from novice to fairly advanced standard. Conformation and action do not play too large a part in these classes, provided the animal is of a reasonable make and shape, but if the judge cannot make up his mind between two animals the one with the better conformation must win the day.

RIDING CLASS

The idea of this class is to judge the ability and style of the rider and the control, or lack of it, that he or she has over the horse rather than the performance or conformation of the horse. Obviously a good-looking, free moving horse will make his 'average' rider look much better than he or she would if riding a straight-shouldered, common sort of animal who has to be pushed on all the time, and the judge has to try to decide whether it is the horse who makes the rider appear better than she is or whether she is in fact a rider with rather more ability than her neighbour. The class may be divided into height and age sections (one for children aged 13 years and under riding ponies of 13·2 h.h. or under and the other for older riders and larger animals) or it may be divided into novice and open sections (for those who have or have not won a first, second or third prize in a similar class prior to the show). Riders are required to walk, trot and canter on both reins, but are not usually required to jump. In addition they are expected to give an individual show including the walk, trot, canter, gallop, circle, halt and rein back. Riding classes appear to be found mainly on the schedules of the Home County shows, and they are always difficult classes to judge.

HANDY HORSE OR PONY

This is a class open to everyone and requires a steady, willing and obedient animal who does a bit of everything. Exhibits are usually judged singly and, depending on the judge, an animal may be asked to do almost anything – which may include opening gates, jumping small fences, backing between straw bales, standing still to be mounted and dismounted from both sides, having an umbrella opened almost under his nose, having his rider pick up sacks, having water from a hose pipe run over his feet, walking through a trailer, or anything else the judge can think up. Exhibits must also of course walk, trot and canter freely on both reins. Conformation is not taken into consideration, the one performing the best test taking the ribbons.

RIDING HORSE

Riding horse classes are similar to hack classes but the same degree of elegance and refinement is not called for. At shows where hack classes are also held, horses are not usually allowed to enter both hack and riding horse classes. This class is open to mares or geldings exceeding 15 h.h. and is judged 50 per cent on conformation, presence and action, and 50 per cent on ride, manners and training. It is judged in the same fashion as a hack class, except that exhibitors may be required, in addition, to gallop, and an individual show, including the walk, trot and canter on both reins, halt and rein back, will be required. A smooth balanced ride and good conformation and action are required. Blemishes are heavily penalised.

BEST CONDITION AND TURNOUT

This class is usually the first of the day since it is purely a
beauty parade and is judged, as its name implies, on the
condition of the animal, the way he is turned out and presented and the cleanness of his tack. He must, for instance,
in order to be considered, have his mane neatly plaited
and his tail either plaited or pulled. The ears and heels
should be trimmed and he should be groomed and wisped
until he shines. The saddle and bridle should be really clean,
with bits and buckles polished; and the rider's dress, too,
should receive careful attention, everything being clean, neat
and tidy.

RIDING CLUB TEAMS

These classes are open to teams of three horses and riders
from riding clubs affiliated to the B.H.S. Riders must be 17
years or over and must be members of the riding club they
represent and the horses must be owned by members of the
club. The class is judged on condition and cleanness of horse
and saddlery, 15 marks being awarded for this section.
Judges examine the saddlery and marks are given for the
cleanness and state of repair. The horse should be clean and
well trimmed and shod. Conformation is not taken into
account. Marks out of 15 are given for the turnout of the
rider, the judges taking into consideration the general cleanness but not the value of the clothes. The rider must be suit-
ably turned out in a bowler hat or riding cap, hunting tie,
dark coat, breeches and boots. Each team is required to give
a short show of their own choice lasting approximately two
minutes. After the show the team is required to canter round
the ring and jump two small fences as a team. Any team that
fails to jump is eliminated. The display is marked out of 50
and the jumping out of a possible 20 marks. Horses should
match or complement each other as far as possible.

A riding club team in action. The riders are all dressed as alike as possible and the horses complement each other.

WESTERN CLASSES

Western classes come under the auspices of the Western Horseman's Association of Great Britain and classes that may be included on the schedule are Western pleasure, Western equitation, stock horse and trail classes. The Western pleasure class is similar to riding horse classes and is judged on conformation, action, ride and manners. The paces required are walk, jog, a steady ground-covering trot, and lope, a slow uncollected canter. Marks are also awarded for the suitability of the horse for the rider. Western equitation classes are judged in the same way as riding classes, marks being awarded for the position, style and ability of the rider. An individual show is also required, all movements being ridden on one hand. Trail classes correspond to the handy pony classes; similar obstacles are negotiated and other tests include stepping through tyres and dragging a pole or sleeper. Stock horse classes are intended to test the horse's ability to work cattle. Competitors are required to perform sliding stops, figures of eight, including a flying change (changing legs at canter without coming back to trot) and quick starts, as well as the walk, jog and lope in both directions. Another class occasionally seen is the versatility class which consists of two parts, the first Western pleasure and the second English hack. The change-over of tack and clothes is done in the arena with a limited time allowance.

Chapter 9

Turnout for Horse and Rider

The horse world is essentially conservative in outlook and the changes in fashion that occur each season in the outside world affect the showing fraternity only slightly. For instance it is only in the last ten years or so that stretch breeches have largely replaced those made of cavalry twill, and far more recently that showing coats of brown, dark green and maroon, all with velvet collars, have made the occasional appearance between the conventionally coloured black and navy ones.

THE RIDER

The accepted show ring dress does, however, vary according to the type of show and the time of day that the class is held. Standard dress for riders in show and working hunter and cob classes at county show level is as follows: Light-coloured (preferably yellow but not white) breeches and black boots should be worn by riders of both sexes. Men wear a collar and tie, tweed coat and bowler hat; the correct dress for ladies is a white stock, black or navy jacket and either a velvet hunting cap or a bowler hat. All riders should wear leather gloves and blunt spurs and should carry a plain or leather-covered showing cane. For evening performances

A line-up of ladies' hacks, ridden side-saddle, at the Royal Windsor Horse Show.

the dress for hunter classes is more formal – top hats and tail coats for ladies and full hunting dress, complete with whip, for men. In hack classes, too, especially those held in the afternoon or evening, dress tends to be more formal and adds to the general impression of elegance given by the horse. At major shows ladies wear light-coloured breeches, black boots, black or navy jacket, white stock with a plain pin, and top hat, with a yellow or red waistcoat just visible under the coat. Formal wear for men consists of morning dress (tail coat, tight black trousers and black boots) with a top hat, a grey cravat and yellow waistcoat. Again leather gloves should be worn and a showing cane carried. At evening performances ladies replace their black coat with a tail coat. At smaller shows, or for morning classes, breeches and boots, black coat, collar and tie and hunting cap are acceptable dress. Side-saddle habits should, of course, be worn in ladies side-saddle hack and hunter classes, a stock and top hat and veil being worn for afternoon and evening performances and a collar and tie and bowler hat and veil being worn for classes held in the morning. If at all possible the hair should be worn in a neat bun at the nape of the neck, especially if a bowler or top hat is worn. Failing this, hair should be worn in a net. In all ridden show and working pony classes the child should wear jodhpurs, black or brown jodhpur boots, preferably with elastic sides, a shirt and tie, black or navy coat and velvet cap. Leather gloves and a showing cane complete the outfit. Spurs are forbidden in all pony classes. Unless the child has plaits, the hair should be put into a hair-net since long flowing locks do nothing to enhance the overall appearance.

What one might call the 'standard county show dress' (breeches, boots, black or navy coat, shirt and tie and hunting cap – or stock and bowler hat – for ladies; tweed coat, collar and tie and bowler hat for men, together with gloves, spurs and showing cane) is the acceptable dress for virtually all other ridden classes. In some classes, particularly those for riding club teams, buttonholes are worn; to look smart they must be small ones, otherwise exhibitors tend to resemble a greenhouse. The keynote to all show classes, however, is cleanliness, tidiness and neatness. The exception to the conventional dress occurs in Western classes where an assortment of clothes can be seen. However, the usual dress is denim jeans, or suede or leather chaps with or without fringes, a plain or coloured shirt with a cravat, Western boots with spurs and a felt Western hat. Dress for driving classes is a matter of personal preference, so long as the outfit is neat, smart and professional-looking, but a hat is a must and so is a driving apron.

In the in-hand classes the exhibitor should be no less neatly dressed than in the ridden classes. A shirt and tie, neatly pressed trousers or jodhpurs, hacking jacket and clean jodhpur boots or flat shoes are suitable for a lady. The hair should be tied back or kept under control by a scarf. A suit and bowler hat is suitable dress for a man.

THE HORSE

All hunters, both show and working, should have their manes plaited and their tails either neatly pulled or plaited. Any excess feather on the heels should be pulled out with the fingers rather than cut with scissors since this gives a neater appearance. The hair on the ears should also be trimmed, and the tail hair banged (cut off square three inches below the hock). Hunters should wear a double bridle, not too narrow, with a plain leather browband and a straight-cut showing saddle to show off the shoulder to better advantage, although an ordinary forward-cut saddle is quite suitable for working hunters when the exhibitor is required to jump. A leather girth, either a balding or three-fold one, should be used for all hunter and cob classes. Cobs should be similarly attired in a plain leather double bridle and straight-cut saddle, but they should always be shown hogged and with their tails pulled. Hacks, show ponies and working hunter ponies should also be shown with plaited manes and pulled or plaited tails, and hacks and show ponies should also wear straight-cut saddles, usually with a white webbing girth, and a narrow stitched leather double bridle, frequently with a velvet or silk covered browband. Working ponies may wear ordinary forward-cut saddles with either double or snaffle bridle. Novice, leading rein and first ridden ponies must only be ridden in snaffles.

Pure-bred Arabians, whether ridden or shown in hand, must not be plaited but must have their manes and tails left free, as must Palominos and Spotted animals. All should wear double bridles. Part-bred and Anglo-Arabs, both in-hand and ridden, should, however, be plaited. All exhibits in the in-hand mountain and moorland classes should be left entirely unplaited except for the Welsh Mountain, Welsh Section C and Welsh Cob who, to be different, are traditionally – but not necessarily – shown with one single plait left long and untied immediately behind the ears. In recent years the New Forest and Welsh Section B has also begun to appear plaited at some shows, but the usual procedure in native classes is for manes and tails to be left free and flowing in their natural state.

Brood mares in in-hand hunter or pony classes are usually shown in a double bridle while foals can wear a leather foal slip. One-, two- or three-year-old hunters and ponies are often shown in leather show headcollars with brass rosettes and fittings and with a snaffle bit attached by leather straps to the D-rings at the side. Hunter and pony stallions should be shown in stallion bridles and native pony stallions, principally the Welsh breeds, are often shown with a roller and side reins. Donkey mares may be shown in a show headcollar, but stallions should wear a stallion bit. Either white web or leather lead reins are suitable for the in-hand exhibitor.

Whatever the class, the horse must be presented in the show ring to the best possible advantage, well muscled and groomed and appearing keen and alert. Wisping (bringing a wisp made of hay, or a stable rubber down with a hard rhythmic series of bangs on to the muscular parts of the horse) can, over a period of time, do wonders to build up muscles in areas where the horse is deficient in this respect. The areas to derive most benefit from this action are the neck and quarters but it must never be practised on the loins, since it can do a deal of damage to the kidneys, which lie under this area. In all classes it is always worthwhile adding the finishing touches to your exhibit. Such things as rubbing a chalk block into white socks for added whiteness, provided of course that it is brushed out again before going into the ring, rubbing boot polish in to disguise the odd white marking or broken knee, oiling the feet both inside and out, and wiping a smear of Vaseline round the eyes and nostrils to give added sparkle, are all part of the 'tricks of the trade' and are expected and accepted as such. Light aluminium shoes or lightweight racing plates are often fitted to hacks and show ponies to enable freer and more active and exaggerated paces. In-hand exhibits can be shown unshod behind, provided that their feet are sufficiently hard and the horn of good enough quality not to break or to wear down too much.

Before leaving this chapter on turnout, mention must be made of show condition. Judging from the animals seen round the shows in recent years, it appears that there is some confusion between show condition and just plain fat. Far too many animals appear in the ring with loaded shoulders and a body which appears too big for the legs to support adequately; this 'overtopped' condition obviously considerably restricts the animal's movement. The ideal show specimen is one who is fit and muscled enough to perform well and to show off his conformation and paces to the best advantage without being either hard, racing fit and 'running up light', or too fat to move. It is a mistaken belief that fatness disguises faults which are impossible to eradicate. It may, but it will create more long-term defects than it ever disguises. A good judge will recognise this and judge accordingly.

Chapter 10

Show Jumping

Although the horse show in its proper sense was never taken to include jumping classes, these have now become so popular, being included in every show bar breed and specialist shows, that mention must be made of them. There is now virtually no closed season for show jumping; a series of indoor jumping shows has sprung up during the winter months in addition to those held outside throughout the summer. The All England Show Jumping Arena at Hickstead, which was founded in 1960, and the more recent Arena North show ground in Lancashire, are the only two grounds to have permanent fixed fences erected in their main arenas. Hickstead's main feature is the 10 ft 6 in. high Hickstead Bank, based on the Hamburg bank, and used annually for the British Jumping Derby.

All the larger shows affiliate their jumping classes to the British Show Jumping Association (B.S.J.A.), an association founded in 1921 with the object of stabilising the rules of judging and of promoting the sport, and their classes are held according to the rules laid down by that body. All riders, both adults and children, competing at affiliated shows must be members or junior members of the B.S.J.A. and their horses registered annually with the Society. Once having joined the Society, no member or his horse can compete at unaffiliated shows, with the exception of ponies under 13·2 h.h.

To be eligible for affiliation, shows have to provide judges who are on the B.S.J.A. list of approved judges and provide

The crowded arena of an indoor jumping show.

at least one practice fence outside the arena. The course itself must be built in accordance with B.S.J.A. rulings. Virtually all national competitions are judged under B.S.J.A. Table A or Table S rules while all international competitions are governed by the F.E.I. rulings, the international body to which the B.S.J.A. and all foreign show jumping bodies are affiliated.

Table S is used for judging speed competitions such as Take Your Own Line. This competition is very similar to Have A Gamble competitions and each fence is allotted a number of marks according to how difficult it is. The object is for the rider to take his own line, jumping the fences – each fence once only – in any order he likes, to get as many marks as possible within a given time limit.

The Scurry competition, too, is judged under Table S and takes place over a medium-sized course of obstacles, no penalties being added for faults incurred but eight seconds being added for each fence knocked down.

Pair Relay is a competition involving two riders and is also judged under Table S. The first rider jumps the medium-sized course in the fastest possible time before handing over a baton to his partner who then jumps the same course. No penalties are awarded for fences knocked down but time faults, 6–10 seconds, are added to the total time taken for riders to complete the course, those finishing in the fastest time being the winners.

Hit and Hurry competitions are also judged on time but the rules are slightly different. Competitors jump as many fences as they can, in the correct order, in one minute and get three marks for each fence cleared in that time and one for each fence knocked down.

Gamblers' Stakes is similar to Take Your Own Line competitions. Obstacles of varying height and difficulty are numbered in accordance with a pack of playing cards (king, queen, jack, etc.) and each has a value of between 10 and 100 marks – the more difficult the fence the higher the mark. Competitors have to jump seven fences of their own choice within a time limit of two minutes and each fence can be jumped as many times as the rider wishes. Competitors who fail to jump the seven fences within the time are eliminated and the object is to get as high a total as possible.

Table A competitions are judged under one of four sections, A1, A2, A3 and A4. Under section A1, prize money is divided when there is equality of faults for first place after a second jump-off; under A2, time is the deciding factor in the second jump-off in the case of equality of faults; under A3, time decides the winner in the first jump-off; and under A4, time decides the winner in the first round. Faults are incurred under both Table A and F.E.I. rules as follows: fence knocked down or foot in the water – 4 (only knocking down the top pole of a fence counts for faults; the dislodgement of a lower pole is not penalised; first refusal or run out at a fence – 3 faults; second refusal or runout at same fence – 6 faults; third refusal or run out at same fence – elimination; fall of horse or rider – 8 faults (the horse is judged to have fallen when its shoulder touches the ground. A quarter of a fault is added for each second taken to complete the course over the time allowed, and in a timed jump-off one fault is incurred for each second over a time, fixed for the course before the competition starts, and known as the time allowed. A competitor can also be eliminated for starting before the bell, taking the wrong course, knocking over the timing equipment, failing to start within one minute of the starting bell, leaving the arena, showing a horse a fence before jumping, receiving unauthorised assistance, not going through the start and finish mounted, and exceeding the time limit (which is usually twice the time allowed).

Horses are graded with the B.S.J.A. according to how much money they have won: Grade C up to £150; Grade B between £150 and £399 and Grade A £400 and over. Ponies are graded JC when they have won up to £74, and JA when their winnings reach £75 and over.

Principal among the Grade C competitions are the Fox-hunter, a competition started in 1954 and named after Col. Harry Llewellyn's great horse of that name, and the Wing Newcomers, a more recent innovation. Foxhunter competitions are designed to encourage novice horses to jump medium-sized, well built obstacles, of no more than 3 ft 9 in. in the first round, and they are open to Grade C horses over 14·2 h.h. who have not won more than £50 and are ridden by adults. These competitions are held on an area basis and the finals are held at the Horse of the Year Show. They are judged under Table A2. The Wing Newcomers is designed, as its name implies, for newcomers to jumping who are over 14·2 h.h. and have won less than £15. This too is judged under Table A2, fences not exceeding 3 ft 3 in. initially, and the competition must be ridden by adults. Popular Open competitions are open to horses of any grade except Grade A horses who have won more than £400 in that grade. Fences initially do not exceed 4 ft 6 in.

Corresponding competitions are held for juniors. Junior Foxhunter competitions are open to JC ponies who have not won a total of £35. Fences do not exceed 3 ft 6 in. in the first round. Junior Popular Open competitions are open to JA ponies and fences do not exceed 3 ft 9 in. in the first round. To compete in junior classes, members must ride ponies not exceeding 14·2 h.h. and a height certificate may be called for. Juniors between 14 and 16 may ride horses in adult competitions and ponies in junior competitions as well by becoming Junior Associate Members, and they are then also entitled to compete in Young Rider competitions.

Over recent years there has been a deal of feeling as to whether top rank show jumpers should be classed as professionals or amateurs, although with the exception of the Olympic Games and the Pan American Games show jumping competitions are open to riders of both categories. An amateur rider is 'any person over 18 who does not attempt to make a profit through competition, and whose main or substantial source of income is not derived from equestrian competition'. A professional may make his living out of buying, selling and training horses and through advertising. To date, however, Britain appears to be the only country to have abided by this definition.

The other recent development is the thorny problem of administering drugs and dope testing, and it has now become a 'specific offence' unreasonably to refuse to allow a horse who has competed or is about to compete in a show jumping competition to undergo any properly authorised test or examination. Whereas this offence has in the past been dealt with by imposing a small fine, competitors are now liable to face periods of prolonged suspension.

Chapter 11

Where to Go –
the Principal Shows

This chapter is intended as a guide to where one is most likely to find the widest and most comprehensive choice of each particular aspect of the show ring. All these shows are held annually.

The pure show classes – ridden hunters, hacks, cobs, show ponies

The Royal Windsor Horse Show, Home Park, Windsor, Berks. Held in May.

The South of England Show, incorporating the Royal Richmond Show, South of England Showground, Ardingly, Sussex. Held in June.

The Royal Show, Royal Agricultural Society Showground, Stoneleigh, Warwicks. Held in July.

The Royal International Horse Show, Empire Pool, Wembley, London. Held in July.

The Royal Dublin Horse Show (hunters), Balls Bridge, Dublin. Held in August.

The Horse of the Year Show, Empire Pool, Wembley, London. Held in October.

Working Hunter Ponies

B.S.P.S. Working Hunter Pony Championships, East of England Showground, Peterborough. Held in September.

Arabians

The Arab Horse Society Show. Held in various venues near to London in July.

The Arab Horse Society's Northern Show, Haydock Park Racecourse. Held in June.

Mountain and Moorland Ponies

National Pony Society's Show, The Three Counties Showground, Malvern, Worcs. Held in August.

The Ponies of Britain Summer Show, The East of England Showground, Peterborough. Held in August.

The Ponies of Britain Stallion Show, Windsor Racecourse, Berks. Held in April.

The Ponies of Britain Scottish Show, Kelso, Roxburghshire. Held in July.

The West Midland Stallion Show, The Three Counties Showground, Malvern. Held in April.

The Royal Windsor Horse Show, Home Park, Windsor, Berks. Held in May.

The Royal Welsh Show (the Welsh breeds), Builth Wells, Powys. Held in July.

The Royal Highland Show (Shetland and Highland ponies), Ingliston, Edinburgh. Held in June.

In addition, most of the breed societies hold their own show and the society secretary will supply information.

Donkeys

The Donkey Breed Society's Championships, National Equestrian Centre, Stoneleigh, Warwicks. Held in September.

Royal Windsor Horse Show, Home Park, Windsor. Held in May.

In-hand Hunters

H.I.S. Stallion Show, Newmarket, Suffolk. Held in March.

H.I.S. Hunter Show, Shrewsbury, Salop. Held in June.

Palominos

British Palomino Society Championships. Held in various
venues in June.

Shires

National Shire Horse Show, East of England Showground,
Peterborough. Held in March.

Clydesdales

Royal Highland Show, Ingliston, Edinburgh. Held in June.

Percherons

British Percheron Society Show. Held in various East
Anglian venues in May.

Suffolks

The Woodbridge Horse Show, Suffolk County Showground,
Ipswich. Held on Easter Monday.

Private Driving

British Driving Society Meet, Smith's Lawn, Windsor,
Berks. Held in June.

Royal Windsor Horse Show, Home Park, Windsor, Berks.
Held in May.

Hackneys

Hackney Breed Society Show, in conjunction with the South
of England Show, Ardingly, Sussex. Held in June.

Double Harness Events

Horse of the Year Show, Wembley. Held in October.

Combined Driving

Royal Windsor Horse Show, Home Park, Windsor, Berks.
Held in May.

National Driving Championships. Held in various venues in July.

Lowther Driving Trials, Lowther Park, Cumbria. Held in August.

Show Jumping

Hickstead All England Jumping Arena, Hickstead, Sussex. Meetings are held four times a year – over Easter, in July, the Derby meeting in August and in September.

Arena North, Charnock Richard, Lancs. Meetings are held four times a year in April, June, August and September.

Cardiff International Show Jumping Championships, Cardiff Castle. Held in June.

Royal International Horse Show, Wembley. Held in July.

Horse of the Year Show, Wembley. Held in October.

International Show Jumping Championships, Olympia, London. Held in December.

Chapter 12

Useful Societies

Arab Horse Society: Lt-Col. J. A. Denney, Sackville Lodge, Lye Green, Crowborough, Sussex.

British Horse Society: J. E. Blackmore, The National Equestrian Centre, Stoneleigh, Kenilworth, Warwicks.

British Show Jumping Association: Lt-Com. W. B. Jefferis, The National Equestrian Centre, Stoneleigh, Kenilworth, Warwicks.

British Driving Society: Mrs. P. Candler, 10 Marley Avenue, New Milton, Hants.

British Palomino Society: Mrs. P. Howell, Kingsettle Stud, Cholderton, Salisbury, Wilts.

British Appaloosa Society: Mrs. D. G. de Rivaz, Woodcock Lodge Farm, Tylers Causeway, nr. Hertford, Herts.

British Show Hack and Cob Association: J. E. Blackmore, The National Equestrian Centre, Stoneleigh, Kenilworth, Warwicks.

British Show Pony Society: Captain R. Grellis, Smale Farm, Wisborough Green, Billingshurst, Sussex.

British Percheron Society: D. G. Mascall, Owen Webb House, Gresham Road, Cambridge.

Clydesdale Horse Society: S. Gilmore, 24 Beresford Terrace, Ayr.

Combined Driving Group: C. Smith, The National Equestrian Centre, Stoneleigh, Kenilworth, Warwicks.

Dales Pony Society: G. H. Hudgson, Ivy House Farm, Yarm-on-Leer, Yorks.

Dartmoor Pony Society: D. W. J. O'Brien, Chelwood Farm, Nutley, Uckfield, Sussex.

Donkey Breed Society: Mrs. M. P. C. Stevenson, White Shutters, Exlade, Woodcote, Reading, Berks.

English Connemara Society: Mrs. Barthorp, The Quinta, Bently, Farnham, Surrey.

Exmoor Pony Society: R. G. Gibbons, Park House, West Porlock, Somerset.

Fell Pony Society: Miss P. Crossland, Packway, Windermere, Cumbria.

Fédération Équestre Internationale: Chevalier H. De Menten de Horne, Avenue Hamoir 38, Brussels 18, Belgium.

Hunters' Improvement and Light Horse Breeding Society: G. W. Evans, National Westminster Bank Chambers, 8 Market Square, Westerham, Kent.

Hackney Horse Society: The Secretary, National Equestrian Centre, Stoneleigh, Kenilworth, Warwicks.

Highland Pony Society: J. McIldowie, Dunblane, Perthshire.

Joint Measurement Scheme: The National Equestrian Centre, Stoneleigh, Kenilworth, Warwicks.

National Pony Society: Commander B. H. Brown, Stoke Lodge, 85 Cliddesden Road, Basingstoke, Hants.

New Forest Pony Breeding and Cattle Society: Miss D. Macnair, Beacon Corner, Burley, Ringwood, Hants.

Ponies of Britain: Mrs. G. Spooner, Brookside Farm, Ascot, Berks.

Riding Clubs' Movement: Miss J. Bennett, National Equestrian Centre, Stoneleigh, Kenilworth, Warwicks.

Shetland Pony Breeders' Stud Book: D. M. Patterson, 8 Whinfield Road, Montrose, Angus.

Shire Horse Society: R. W. Bird, East of England Showground, Alwalton, Peterborough.

Suffolk Horse Society: c/o 6 Church Street, Woodbridge, Suffolk.

Welsh Pony and Cob Society: T. E. Roberts, 6 Chalybeate Street, Aberystwyth, Dyfed SY23 1HS.

Western Horseman's Association of Great Britain: Mrs. H. Aylward, 3 Church Style Cottages, Stoodleigh, Tiverton, Devon.

Weatherby and Sons: Wellingborough, Northamptonshire, NN8 4BX.

Index